GW00722488

Blackstone's
Police Q& A

Crime 2007

Blackstone's
Police Q&A

Crime 2007

Fifth edition

Huw Smart and John Watson

OXFORD
UNIVERSITY PRESS

OXFORD

UNIVERSITY PRESS

Great Clarendon Street, Oxford OX2 6DP

Oxford University Press is a department of the University of Oxford.
It furthers the University's objective of excellence in research, scholarship,
and education by publishing worldwide in

Oxford New York

Auckland Bangkok Buenos Aires Cape Town Chennai
Dar es Salaam Delhi Hong Kong Istanbul Karachi Kolkata
Kuala Lumpur Madrid Melbourne Mexico City Mumbai Nairobi
São Paulo Shanghai Taipei Tokyo Toronto

With offices in

Argentina Austria Brazil Chile Czech Republic France Greece
Guatemala Hungary Italy Japan Poland Portugal Singapore
South Korea Switzerland Thailand Turkey Ukraine Vietnam

Published in the United States
by Oxford University Press Inc., New York

© Huw Smart and John Watson, 2007

The moral rights of the authors have been asserted

Crown copyright material is reproduced under Class Licence
Number C01P0000148 with the permission of OPSI
and the Queen's Printer for Scotland

Database right Oxford University Press (maker)

First published 2007

All rights reserved. No part of this publication may be reproduced,
stored in a retrieval system, or transmitted, in any form or by any means,
without the prior permission in writing of Oxford University Press,
or as expressly permitted by law, or under terms agreed with the appropriate
reprographics rights organization. Enquiries concerning reproduction
outside the scope of the above should be sent to the Rights Department,
Oxford University Press, at the address above

You must not circulate this book in any other binding or cover
and you must impose this same condition on any acquirer

British Library Cataloguing in Publication Data

Data available

Library of Congress Cataloging in Publication Data

Data available

Typeset by Laserwords Private Limited, Chennai, India
Printed in Great Britain
on acid-free paper by
Ashford Colour Press Limited, Gosport, Hampshire

ISBN 0-19-920336-9   978-0-19-920336-9

10 9 8 7 6 5 4 3 2 1

Contents

Introduction

Before you get into the detail of this book, there are two myths about multiple-choice questions (MCQs) that we need to get out of the way right at the start:

1. that they are easy to answer;
2. that they are easy to write.

Take one look at a professionally designed and properly developed exam paper such as those used by the Police Promotion Examinations Board or the National Board of Medical Examiners in the US and the first myth collapses straight away. Contrary to what some people believe, MCQs are not an easy solution for examiners and not a 'multiple-guess' soft option for examinees.

That is not to say that *all* MCQs are taxing, or even testing — in the psychometric sense. If MCQs are to have any real value at all, they need to be carefully designed and follow some agreed basic rules.

And this leads us to myth number 2.

It is widely assumed by many people and educational organisations that anyone with the knowledge of a subject can write MCQs. You need only look at how few MCQ writing courses are offered by training providers in the UK to see just how far this myth is believed. Similarly, you need only to have a go at a few badly designed MCQs to realise that it is a myth none the less. Writing bad MCQs is easy; writing good ones is no easier than answering them!

As with many things, the design of MCQs benefits considerably from time, training and experience. Many MCQ writers fall easily and often unwittingly into the trap of making their questions too hard, too easy or too obscure, or completely different from the type of question that you will eventually encounter in your own particular exam. Others seem to use the MCQ as a way to catch people out or to show how smart they, the authors, are (or think they are).

There are several purposes for which MCQs are very useful. The first is in producing a reliable, valid and fair test of knowledge and understanding across a wide range of subject matter. Another is an aid to study, preparation and revision for such examinations and tests. The differences in objective mean that there are slight differences in the rules that the MCQ writers follow. Whereas the design of fully validated MCQs is to be used in high stakes examinations which will effectively determine who passes and who fails have very strict guidelines as to construction, content and style, less stringent rules apply to MCQs that are being used for teaching and revision. For that reason, there may be types of MCQ that are appropriate in the latter setting which would not be used in the former. However, in developing the MCQs for this book, the authors have tried to follow the fundamental rules of MCQ design but they would not claim to have replicated the level of psychometric rigour that is — and has to be — adopted by the type of examining bodies referred to above.

These MCQs are designed to reinforce your knowledge and understanding, to highlight any gaps or weaknesses in that knowledge and understanding and to help focus your revision of the relevant topics.

I hope that we have achieved that aim.

Good luck!

Blackstone's Police Q&As — Special Features

References to Blackstone's Police Manuals

Every answer is followed by a paragraph reference to Blackstone's Police Manuals. This means that once you have attempted a question and looked at an answer, the Manual can immediately be referred to for help and clarification.

Unique numbers for each question

Each question and answer has the same unique number. This should ensure that there is no confusion as to which question is linked to which answer. For example, Question 2.1 is linked to Answer 2.1.

Checklists

The checklists are designed to help you keep track of your progress when answering the multiple choice questions. If you fill in the checklist after attempting a question, you will be able to check how many you got right on the first attempt and will know immediately which questions need to be revisited a second time. Please visit www.blackstonespolicemanuals.com and click through to the Blackstone's Police Q&As 2007 page. You will then find electronic versions of the checklists to download and print out. Email any queries or comments on the book to: police.uk@oup.com

Acknowledgements

This book has been written as an accompaniment to *Blackstone's Police Manuals*, and will test the knowledge you have accrued through reading that series. It is of the essence that full study of the relevant chapters in each *Police Manual* is completed prior to attempting the Questions and Answers. As qualified police trainers we recognise that students tend to answer questions incorrectly either because they don't read the question properly, or because one of the 'distracters' has done its work. The distracter is one of the three incorrect answers in a multiple choice question (MCQ), and is designed to distract you from the correct answer and in this way discriminate between candidates: the better-prepared candidate not being 'distracted'.

So particular attention should be paid to the *Answers* sections, and students should ask themselves 'Why did I get that question wrong?' and, just as importantly, 'Why did I get that question right?' Combining the information gained in the *Answers* section together with re-reading the chapter in the *Police Manuals* should lead to greater understanding of the subject matter.

The authors wish to thank Katie at Oxford University Press for her support, patience and cajoling skills! Thanks also to Geraldine Mangley at OUP for her invaluable assistance. We would also like to show appreciation to Alistair MacQueen for his vision and support, without which this project would never have been started.

Huw would like to thank both Julie and their beautiful baby Hâf, for their constant strength and support during long evenings and weekends of writing, when he could have been having fun with the family.

John would like to thank Sue for her support; also David, Catherine and Andrew for not too many 'Dad can I have the computer please!. . . '

1 | State of Mind and Criminal Conduct

STUDY PREPARATION

This chapter, which combines two chapters from the Blackstone's Manuals, tests what could be best described as the general principles of criminal law. When you consider that to prove its case, the prosecution must always prove 'the facts in issue' (*Evidence & Procedure Manual*) beyond a reasonable doubt, then knowledge of the *actus reus* and the *mens rea* becomes very important. In this chapter we will look at the general rule that an offence can be committed only where criminal conduct is accompanied by some element of fault and that both elements must coincide at the same moment in time. The precise fault element required depends upon the particular offence involved, as well as the fact that there is nevertheless a class of offences of 'strict liability', in which no fault element need be proved. In such cases, one can therefore have an *actus reus* without any corresponding *mens rea*. Also tested will be behaviours associated with criminal acts, both by one defendant and also other accessories. When answering questions in this chapter you should remember that although they are based on substantive offences committed, they are testing the general principles of criminal law.

QUESTIONS

Question 1.1

LAWRENCE hates his wife and plans to kill her. He intends to cut her throat on Tuesday morning whilst she is still asleep. On Monday, LAWRENCE picks his wife up from work and is driving home; he is deep in thought about the following day's planned action. Owing to his inattentiveness, LAWRENCE drives through a red light, and his car is struck on his wife's side. She dies as a result of the accident.

Could LAWRENCE be guilty of murder in these circumstances?
A Yes, as he has achieved his desired outcome.
B Yes, as he was thinking about the murder at the time of the accident.
C No, he cannot be guilty of murder in these circumstances.
D No, but he could be guilty of manslaughter.

Question 1.2

ORMEROD had been lawfully arrested by an officer for being in possession of coun-terfeit currency. Due to being violent the officer had placed handcuffs on ORMEROD and still had the counterfeit currency in his hand. ORMEROD saw her opportunity to destroy the evidence and tried to snatch the note out the officer's hand using her mouth and teeth. During this action she bit the officer on the hand, drawing blood.

Considering the concept of 'recklessness' has ORMEROD committed an assault on the police officer?
A Yes, as there was an obvious risk of contact with the officer's hand and the de-fendant took that risk.
B Yes, as the defendant was reckless as to the extent of injury she might have inflicted on the officer.
C No, the assault was committed accidentally; there was no intention to injure the officer.
D No, the defendant was not reckless as to whether she injured the officer; she was reckless as to whether she would destroy the evidence.

Question 1.3

A few, relatively rare offences can be committed by 'negligence'.
In relation to the term 'negligence', which of the following statements is cor-rect?
A Negligence is concerned with the defendant's standards.
B Negligence is concerned with the defendant's state of mind.
C Negligence is concerned with standards of a reasonable person.
D Negligence is concerned with standards of the law as laid down in statute.

Question 1.4

WHITE was broke and anxious to inherit his mother's money. One night he put potassium cyanide in his mother's bedtime drink with the intention of killing her.

In due course, the following morning, it was discovered that his mother had died. WHITE was arrested on suspicion of murder. In fact, WHITE's mother had drunk very little; certainly, nowhere near enough to kill her. She had died of natural causes.

In relation to this, which of the following is true?

A WHITE is guilty of murder as there is a causal link between his actions and his mother's death.

B WHITE is not guilty of any offences as his mother died of natural causes.

C WHITE is guilty of attempted murder due to his intention.

D WHITE is guilty of attempted murder due to his actions, irrespective of his intentions.

Question 1.5

Companies which are 'legally incorporated' have a legal personality of their own.

In relation to companies' liability for an offence, which of the following statements is correct?

A A company could be held liable for an offence, but only if the offence is triable summarily.

B An employer cannot be prosecuted for offences committed by his or her employees, as offences are restricted to personal liability.

C A company cannot be prosecuted where an offence requires *mens rea*.

D A company can be prosecuted for an offence which involves strict liability, or where an offence requires *mens rea*.

Question 1.6

JENKINS was in a crowded pub and was larking about with her friends. She decided to throw a pint of beer over her friend BRYANT. Unfortunately the glass slipped out of her hand and smashed in BRYANT's face, causing cuts which required stitches.

In relation to assault occasioning actual bodily harm, what must be proved?

A Intention to commit any type of assault.

B Intention to cause the actually caused.

C Recklessness as to the assault itself.

D Recklessness as to the injury actually caused.

Question 1.7

MATHERS was on his way to hospital to have his appendix removed. JIANIKOS has long had a hatred of MATHERS and sees him just outside the hospital. JIANIKOS punches MATHERS on the head, not that hard. MATHERS, however, has a very weak skull (JIANIKOS had no knowledge of this), and as a result of the blow suffers a serious head injury. The head injury is not life threatening, but the doctors are unable to operate on him. MATHERS' appendix bursts due to this delay in operating, and as a result he dies.

In relation to causation, which of the following is true?

A JIANIKOS has caused the death of MATHERS because of the punch he gave him.
B JIANIKOS has caused the death of MATHERS because there was no intervening act.
C JIANIKOS has not caused the death of MATHERS; there is no link between the punch and the death.
D JIANIKOS has not caused the death of MATHERS, as he had no knowledge of his weak skull.

Question 1.8

ANDREWS was employed to operate a level crossing on a railway whilst a fault with the automated system was repaired. While at work, ANDREWS called his girlfriend on his mobile phone. He was so engrossed in the conversation that he forgot to close the crossing gates when a train was coming. A car was crossing at the time and the train hit it, killing the driver.

Is ANDREWS criminally liable in the death of the driver of the car?

A No, there was no positive action by ANDREWS to cause the accident.
B Yes, he had failed to carry out his duty and is criminally liable.
C No, ANDREWS did not have the relevant *mens rea*.
D Yes, as there is a causal link between his actions and their consequences.

Question 1.9

MILLAR intends to commit a burglary at a local electrical goods shop. He confides in NEWTON, who suggests he does it at 4 a.m. when it will be quieter, and suggests that MILLAR goes through a skylight into a room that is not alarmed. MILLAR thanks him for his advice and goes ahead with the burglary.

What is NEWTON's liability, if any, for the burglary?

A As a counsellor of the offence.
B As a procurer of the offence.
C As a principal offender of the offence.
D He is not liable at all for the offence.

Question 1.10

BALDWIN intends to murder his wife's lover by shooting him. He goes to see BOOKER, whom he knows to be an illegal gun supplier. BALDWIN tells BOOKER what he intends to do, and asks him to supply a gun. BOOKER is unconcerned whether the murder is successful or not, and is only interested in his profit from the deal. BALDWIN commits the murder, but is caught and tells the police about BOOKER.

Is BOOKER an accessory to the murder?
A No, he does not have the required *mens rea*.
B No, as he has no intention of aiding the actual shooting.
C Yes, he is reckless as to whether the shooting will happen or not.
D Yes, he is an accessory to the murder, as he knows the circumstances.

Question 1.11

JONES is a soldier living in the company barracks. JONES has a fight with STEYN during which he stabs him twice in the stomach with a bayonet. Realising the seriousness of STEYN's injuries, two other soldiers carry him to the nearby medical centre. STEYN is a large man and, due to his heavy weight, the soldiers drop him three times on way to the medical centre. On one of those occasions, STEYN hits his head very hard on the ground. On arrival at the centre, the overworked doctor fails to notice that STEYN's lung has collapsed and the treatment he receives from the doctor is less than adequate. STEYN dies from a culmination of all the injuries and the mistreatment he received.

Given the way STEYN was treated after his injury, is JONES criminally liable for STEYN's death?
A Yes, the chain of causation is not broken.
B No, due to the intervening act of the other soldiers.
C No, due to the intervening act of the doctor.
D Yes, provided the stab wound was the major cause of death.

Question 1.12

MURRAY is one of a gang of armed robbers who rob people in their own houses. They plan to go to GRAHAM's house and rob him. MURRAY is aware that knives will be carried, although he will not carry one himself. MURRAY is also aware that the knives may be used for violence, and that the rest of the gang is violent. During the robbery GRAHAM tries to fight back and is stabbed by one of the gang. GRAHAM dies as a result of his injuries.

In order to show that MURRAY is guilty of murder through joint enterprise, what would have to be proved?

A MURRAY agreed to kill, using the knives.

B MURRAY agreed to cause really serious injury using the knives.

C MURRAY agreed to use knives for any purpose.

D MURRAY contemplated that the knife could be used to cause serious bodily injury.

Question 1.13

PIERCE wished to scare a business rival and recruited two persons to carry out his wishes using a loaded firearm. Unfortunately one of the hired men lost his nerve and shot the male, who died of his injuries.

As the secondary party to the killing, what would need to be shown for PIERCE to be liable for manslaughter as a 'joint enterprise'?

A That the secondary party had an agreement, even tacitly, that the primary party would do what he had done.

B That the secondary party had a clear agreement that the primary party would do what he had done.

C That the secondary party had foreseen the possibility that the primary party would do what he had done.

D That the secondary party could have *reasonably* foreseen the possibility that the primary party would do what he had done.

Question 1.14

'Recklessness' is an important concept in proving certain criminal offences. Which of the following best describes, legally, what is meant by recklessness?

A They were aware a risk did exist; in the circumstances known to them they unreasonably took the risk.

B They were aware a risk did or would exist; in the circumstances known to them they unreasonably took the risk.

C They were aware a risk did exist, it was an obvious risk, and they unreasonably took the risk.

D They were aware a risk did or would exist, it was an obvious risk, and they unreasonably took the risk.

Question 1.15

CROFT and RIGBY were in dispute over £40,000 drugs money owed to RIGBY. RIGBY intended sending out a message to the dealers in the area and decided to kill CROFT. He approached his friend BRYCE, who he knew owned a firearm. BRYCE loaned RIGBY a pistol, suspecting that he would use it to kill CROFT.

If RIGBY were to carry out his plan, what else would the prosecution need to prove, in order to show that this was a joint venture between RIGBY and BRYCE?

A That BRYCE intended assisting RIGBY, and that his actions actually assisted in the commission of the crime.

B That BRYCE actually knew that RIGBY would kill CROFT, and that he approved of the commission of the offence.

C Only that the act was committed by RIGBY, nothing further needs to be proved.

D Only that BRYCE intended to assist RIGBY in the act, regardless of whether his actions actually assisted in the commission of the crime.

Question 1.16

SHEPPARD has been charged with wilful neglect of a child under s. 1 of the Children and Young Persons Act 1933. SHEPPARD's 3-year-old daughter was found to be suffering from severe malnutrition and the prosecution alleges that SHEPPARD failed to provide adequate food and medical aid for her.

In relation to the term 'wilful', what must the prosecution show in respect of SHEPPARD's state of mind, in order to prove this offence?

A That SHEPPARD intended the child to be ill as a result of not feeding her, or providing medical aid.

B That SHEPPARD intended the child to be ill as a result of not feeding her, or providing medical aid, or at least foresaw that this would happen.

1. State of Mind and Criminal Conduct

C That SHEPPARD had considered the consequences of not feeding her, or providing medical aid and intended those consequences to happen.
D That SHEPPARD was aware of the risk but took it anyway due to not caring whether the child's health was at risk or not.

ANSWERS

Answer 1.1

Answer **C** — Murder is a crime of specific intent, and requires a specific *mens rea*, i.e. an intention to kill or seriously injure. To be guilty of a criminal offence requiring *mens rea*, an accused must possess that *mens rea* when performing the act or omission in question, and it must relate to that particular act or omission. If, for example, a man accidentally kills his wife in a car crash on Monday, the fact that he was planning to cut her throat on Tuesday does not make him guilty of her murder (which makes answer A wrong), even if he was thinking about the planned murder at the time of the accident (making answer B incorrect), and even if he is subsequently delighted to find that his wife has died. Similarly, he could not be guilty of manslaughter (answer D) which also requires a specific *mens rea*.

Crime, para. 1.1.3.1

Answer 1.2

Answer **A** — Consider the statutory expressions that exist in English law; the more common expressions are:

- intent
- recklessness
- wilfully
- dishonestly

Looking at the differences between intent and recklessness then an advantage of recklessness over intention is that the former is easier to prove by the attendant circumstances; a disadvantage is the different elements attributed to the word 'reckless' by different courts considering different offences.

An example of this dilemma occurs in *D v DPP* [2005] Crim LR 962. A police officer attended a domestic incident involving a dispute as to the defendant's access to his newborn daughter. The defendant was outside the property. He was arrested to prevent a breach of the peace. When he had calmed down he was allowed to see his daughter. He then ran away pursued by the officer to his home address. During a subsequent struggle the defendant bit the officer on the left hand. The defendant was arrested for assaulting a police constable. He was charged with an offence contrary to s. 89 of the Police Act 1996. The justices found that the defendant was guilty of assaulting the officer by biting him, on the basis that the defendant's actions were reckless. The defendant appealed, arguing that a bite could not be reckless; either it was deliberate or it was accidental.

The Divisional Court held, dismissing the appeal, the test of recklessness in an assault of this kind involved foresight of the risk that the complainant would be subjected to unlawful force and the taking of that risk, that state of mind being coincident with the act of biting. In this scenario the defendant would have realised that a reckless battery might be inflicted using teeth to try to snatch something from the hand of the officer restraining her, being aware that she might make contact with the officer's hand in the process. In these circumstances the defendant would be guilty of a 'reckless' assault and could not argue that its was accidental, or that the recklessness amounted only to whether they would snatch the evidence; answers C and D are therefore incorrect.

The courts have also held that assault occasioning actual bodily harm only requires proof of recklessness as to the assault and there is no need to show that the defendant was reckless as to the extent of the harm caused by his/her assault (see *R v Savage* [1992] 1 AC 699). In this scenario the case would be decided on the recklessness as to the assault itself and not the recklessness as to the injury likely to be caused, and for this reason answer B is incorrect.

Crime, para. 1.1.4.2

Answer 1.3

Answer **C** — Some would exclude negligence from a discussion of *mens rea* on the basis that *mens rea* is concerned with states of mind and negligence is not a state of mind (answer B is incorrect) but is rather a failure to comply with the standards of the reasonable person. Unlike strict liability, negligence still ascribes some notion of 'fault' or 'blame' to the defendant who must be shown to have acted in a way that runs contrary to the expectations of the reasonable person. A good example would be that of careless driving: in *Simpson* v *Peat* [1952] 2 QB 24, it was stated that if a driver was 'exercising the degree of care and attention which a reasonable prudent driver would exercise, he ought not to be convicted' of careless driving. It does not matter what the accused actually believes; it is what the reasonable person in the circumstances would have believed which counts (answer A is incorrect). Nor is it the standards laid down by law in statutes (answer D is incorrect).

Crime, para. 1.1.3.3

Answer 1.4

Answer **C** — There are two primary factors to any crime the *mens rea* and the *actus reus*. The mental element, or intention, is vital and there is a presumption that *mens rea* is required for a criminal offence unless parliament clearly indicates otherwise (*B (A minor)* v *DPP* [2000] 2 WLR 452). Therefore, answer D is incorrect. The relevant *mens rea* for attempted murder is intention to kill. WHITE has also taken action by poisoning the drink. However, where *actus reus* is proved, you must show a causal link between that and the relevant consequences. Despite his best efforts she had died, coincidentally, of natural causes. WHITE's conduct had not in any sense contributed to this and he is not guilty of murder (*R* v *White* [1910] 2 KB 124). Therefore, answer A is incorrect. Had he waited just one more day, there would be no criminal liability upon him. However, his intentions together with his actions make him guilty of attempted murder; therefore, answer B is incorrect.

Crime, paras 1.2.2.2, 1.2.4

Answer 1.5

Answer **D** — This question addresses the issues of corporate liability. Companies have been successfully prosecuted for offences involving strict liability (*Alphacell Ltd* v *Woodward* [1972] AC 824) as well as offences which require *mens rea* (*Tesco Supermarkets Ltd* v *Nattrass* [1972] AC 153), making answer C incorrect. Liability is not limited to summary offences (making answer A incorrect), and companies can be liable for the actions of some of their employees under certain circumstances (making answer B incorrect).

Crime, para. 1.2.7

Answer 1.6

Answer **C** — An assault or battery must be committed intentionally or recklessly, so the least you have to prove is recklessness, not necessarily actual intent (making answers A and B incorrect). If injury is caused, it need not even be proved that the injury was foreseeable. This is now clear from the decision of the House of Lords in *R* v *Savage* [1992] 1 AC 699, in which S aimed to throw the contents of a beer glass over B, but inadvertently allowed the glass to slip from her hand and break, with the result that B was injured by it. A conviction for an offence under s. 47 of the Offences Against the Person Act 1861 could be successful, because throwing beer over B was an intentional assault (indeed a battery) and that same assault had resulted in B's injury. Therefore recklessness as to the assault is all that is needed — not recklessness as to the extent of the harm likely to be caused (making answer D incorrect).

Crime, para. 1.1.4.2

Answer 1.7

Answer **A** — Although legal causation must be 'operative and substantial', it need not necessarily be a direct cause of the proscribed result. In *R v McKechnie* [1992] Crim LR 194, a man inflicted serious head injuries on another man. These were not in themselves fatal, but they prevented doctors from operating on the injured man's duodenal ulcer, and he died when the ulcer burst. The perpetrator was held to have caused his death. There was a link, therefore answer C is incorrect. In what is known colloquially as the 'Eggshell Skull' rule, a person must ordinarily take his victim as he finds him. If, for example, the victim of an assault is unusually vulnerable to physical injury as a result of an existing medical condition or old age, the person responsible must accept liability for any unusually serious consequences which result. This is true particularly where a blow is struck; answer D is therefore incorrect. In relation to intervening acts, no such intervening act can break the chain of causation if it merely complements or aggravates the ongoing effects of the defendant's initial conduct. The chain of causation can be broken only where the effect of the intervening act is so overwhelming that any initial injuries are completely unconnected to the end result, therefore answer B is incorrect.

Crime, para. 1.2.4

Answer 1.8

Answer **B** — Most offences require a positive act, together with the requisite state of mind for the offence to be complete. However, some offences are brought about by a failure to act, and most of these arise from some sort of duty to act (this makes answers A and C incorrect). A person may in some cases incur criminal liability through failure to discharge his official duties or contractual obligations. A typical example is provided by *R v Pittwood* (1902) 19 TLR 37, in which P was employed to operate a level crossing on a railway but omitted to close the crossing gates when a train was signalled. P was convicted of gross negligence manslaughter. It is not a causal link which requires proof that the consequences would not have happened 'but for' the defendant's actions of omission; here, had the train been even one minute late, the accident would not have happened (answer D is also incorrect).

Crime, para. 1.2.3

Answer 1.9

Answer **A** — A principal offender must meet all the requirements of the particular offence, and for procurement there must be a causal link between his conduct and the offence. Counselling requires no causal link (*R* v *Calhaem* [1985] QB 808); all that is required is the principal offender's awareness of the counsellor's advice or encouragement — and this is true even if the principal would have committed the offence anyway (*Attorney General* v *Able* [1984] QB 795). So he is guilty as a counsellor, not as a principal or procurer (making answers B, C and D incorrect).

Crime, para. 1.2.6

Answer 1.10

Answer **D** — One of the leading cases on the state of mind for accessories is *National Coal Board* v *Gamble* [1959] 1 QB 11, where Devlin J at p. 20 stated: '... aiding and abetting is a crime that requires proof of *mens rea*, that is to say, of intention to aid as well as of knowledge of the circumstances'. However, as Devlin J went on to point out, at p. 23, intention to aid does not require that the accused's purpose or motive must be that the principal offence should be committed:

> If one man deliberately sells to another a gun to be used for murdering a third, he may be indifferent about whether the third man lives or dies and interested only in the cash profit to be made out of the sale, but he can still be an aider and abettor. To hold otherwise would be to negative the rule that *mens rea* is a matter of intent only and does not depend on desire or motive.

There must also be an intention to aid the principal offender, and as such recklessness and negligence are not enough to convict an accessory. Thus, answers A, B and C are incorrect.

Crime, para. 1.2.6.1

Answer 1.11

Answer **A** — A defendant will not be regarded as having caused the consequence for which he stands accused if there was a new intervening act sufficient to break the chain of causation between his original action and the consequence in question — in this case the death of STEYN. The chain of causation can be broken only where the effect of the intervening act is so overwhelming that any initial injuries are relegated to the status of mere historical background. In the leading case of *R v Smith* [1959] 2 QB 35, which broadly follows the circumstances outlined in the question, the Courts-Martial Appeals Court held:

> If at the time of death the original wound is still an operating cause and a substantial cause, then the death can properly be said to be the result of the wound, albeit that some other cause of death is also operating. Only if it can be said that the original wounding is merely the setting in which another cause operates can it be said that the death did not result from the wound. Putting it another way, only if the second cause is so overwhelming as to make the original wound merely part of the history can it be said that the death does not flow from the wound.

It follows that a conviction could still be secured. Answers B, C and D are incorrect.

Crime, para. 1.2.5

Answer 1.12

Answer **D** — The main features that will determine MURRAY's liability as an accessory in a joint enterprise will be:

- The nature and extent of the agreed offence.
- Whether the accessory knew the principal had a knife.
- Whether a different knife was used.
- Whether the knife was used differently than agreed.

Proof of prior knowledge of the actual crime intended is not necessary if he contemplated the commission of one of a limited number of crimes by the principal, and intentionally assisted in their commission. For an accessory to be found guilty of murder as a joint enterprise it is not necessary for the prosecution to prove that the principal would kill; it is sufficient to prove that he might kill. The accessory, however, will not be guilty where the lethal act carried out by the principal is fundamentally different from the acts foreseen or intended by the accessory: *R v Powell* [1999] 1 AC 1.

It is therefore enough that MURRAY contemplated that knives might be used, and that no actual agreement needs to be reached by the parties to the crime; therefore, answers A, B and C are incorrect.

Crime, para. 1.2.6.2

Answer 1.13

Answer **C** — This particular area of law is complicated by various factors, particularly when one party is not present at the scene of the crime so to speak. Enormous problems have been encountered where one person involved in a joint venture goes beyond that which was agreed or contemplated by the other(s).

Fortunately for students of the law the Court of Appeal has confirmed the law in relation to joint enterprise in *Attorney General's Reference (No. 3 of 2004)* [2005] EWCA Crim 1882. It was alleged that the defendant had recruited two co-defendants to scare someone with a loaded firearm but one of the co-defendants subsequently went on to shoot the victim dead. The issue turned on whether the first defendant could be convicted of manslaughter on the facts. The primary question raised by the Attorney General was whether a secondary party to a joint enterprise was guilty of manslaughter if he had contemplated an unlawful act to frighten the victim and the principal carried out that act with the necessary intention for murder.

The Court held that test was whether the secondary party had foreseen the possibility that the primary party would do what he had done. In this case the act done by the primary party (shooting the victim) was of a fundamentally different character from any act contemplated by the person who had recruited him — he had not foreseen the possibility of any harm to the victim, let alone any intentional harm. These principles were in accordance with *R v Powell* [1999] 1 AC 1 which was to be regarded as representing the law.

There is no need to have an agreement, tacitly or otherwise; answers A and B are therefore incorrect. And the secondary party's foresight does not have to be reasonable; answer D is therefore incorrect.

Crime, para. 1.2.6.2

Answer 1.14

Answer **B** — There have been decades of complex differences between objective and subjective recklessness; thankfully the law has now been clarified. In *R v G & R* [2003] 3 WLR 1060, the House of Lords decided that objective recklessness (known as *Caldwell* decisions as set out in *Metropolitan Police Commissioner v Caldwell* [1982] AC 341) should be departed from. Their Lordships held that a person acts recklessly (in a criminal damage case):

- With respect to a *circumstance*, when he or she is aware of a risk that exists or would exist.
- With respect to a *result or consequence*, when he or she is aware of a risk that it would occur and it is, in the circumstances known to him or her, unreasonable to take the risk.

This removes the 'it would be obvious to any reasonable bystander' test, therefore answers C and D are incorrect. Also it is more than knowledge that a risk existed; it extends to awareness that a risk would exist — answer A is therefore incorrect.

Crime, para. 1.1.4.2

Answer 1.15

Answer **A** — The issue of joint enterprise normally arises in circumstances, for example, when more than one person is present at the scene of the offence and one person commits an offence (the principal offender), and another is present at the scene, but does not physically take part (the accessory).

The issue is more complicated when the accessory is *not* present during the substantive offence. In *R v Bryce* [2004] 2 Cr App R 35, it was decided that in such cases, the prosecution will need to show *intentional assistance* by the accessory and in order to do this, they would need to prove:

- an act was done by the accessory;
- the act *in fact* assisted the later commission of the offence;
- that the accessory did the act deliberately, realising that it was capable of assisting the offence;
- that the accessory, at the time of doing the act, contemplated the commission of the offence by the principal offender (e.g. he/she foresaw it as a real or substantial risk or real possibility); *and*
- when doing the act the accessory *intended* assisting the principal offender

Dealing with the answers above, the prosecution would not be required to show that BRYCE *knew* that RIGBY would kill CROFT; merely that he *contemplated the commission of the offence*. Also, his *approval* is irrelevant according to the *Bryce* case. Answer B is therefore incorrect. Answer C is incorrect, because the prosecution would need to show more proof than the fact that a firearm was loaned by the accessory to the principal offender (although this would count as evidence in the case). Answer D is incorrect, because the prosecution must show that the accessory's actions actually assisted in the commission of the crime.

Crime, para. 1.2.6.2

Answer 1.16

Answer **D** — The term 'wilfully' is *not* restricted to occasions where a defendant must be shown to have desired the consequences of his/her actions or at least to have foreseen or considered them (*subjective* recklessness). Answers A, B and C are therefore incorrect as they relate to a positive intent to bring about consequences.

The leading case is *R* v *Sheppard* [1981] AC 394, which found that the term will include *objective* recklessness (see the decision of the House of Lords in *R* v *G & R* [2003] 3 WLR 1060). In *Sheppard*, Lord Diplock provided a model direction as follows:

> '... on a charge of wilful neglect of a child under section 1 of the Children and Young Persons Act 1933 by failing to provide adequate medical aid ...the jury must be satisfied (1) that the child did in fact need medical aid at the time at which the parent is charged with failing to provide it (the *actus reus*) and (2) either that the parent was aware at that time that the child's health might be at risk if it were not provided with medical aid, or that the parent's unawareness of this fact was due to his not caring whether his child's health were at risk or not (the *mens rea*)'.

Crime, para. 1.1.4.3

2 Incomplete Offences and Police Investigations

STUDY PREPARATION

Having looked at the key building blocks of *mens rea* and *actus reus*, you now need to go on to consider specific criminal offences and their constituent parts. Before doing so, however, you need to get a few problematic situations out of the way.

The first of these deals with those occasions where the defendant, despite his or her best or worst endeavours, fails to do what he or she set out to do. These are 'incomplete' offences. The second area deals with defences to criminal charges — these are addressed in the next chapter.

When dealing with incomplete offences there are two key things to remember: first, that the physical impossibility of actually achieving what the defendant set out to do will not absolve him or her from criminal liability (and why should it?); and secondly, that some offences — such as summary offences and some incomplete offences themselves — cannot be attempted.

Finally, in this chapter we deal with the related area of police operations, where the evidential and substantive issues often overlap with those of the incomplete offences involved.

QUESTIONS

Question 2.1

It is an offence unlawfully to incite another to commit an offence, and this is an offence contrary to common law.

In relation to the offence of incitement, which of the following is correct?

A The offence is complete where the person incited forms the relevant intention to commit the substantive offence.

B The offence is complete where the person incited commits the substantive offence.

C The person incited must commit the offence due to pressure from the defendant.

D The person incited must be capable of committing the substantive offence that is prompted by the defendant.

Question 2.2

LANTZOS has been charged with an offence of statutory conspiracy under s. 1 of the Criminal Law Act 1977. He has been charged in respect of an agreement with others to commit a summary offence.

How, if at all, is this case likely to be dealt with?

A Withdrawn because you can only conspire to commit an indictable offence.

B Trial at magistrates' court only.

C Trial at Crown Court only.

D Trial at either magistrates' court or Crown Court.

Question 2.3

JANE and JOHN RICE are married. They plan for JOHN to defraud his insurance company over the reported theft of his car. They involve PEARD in their plan by asking him to hide JOHN's car in his garage until the insurance company pay out. However, a few hours before the plan is initiated, PEARD said he did not want to be involved and the RICEs gave up the idea.

Who, if anyone, is guilty of conspiracy to defraud the insurance company?

A No one as the offence contemplated did not take place.

B No one as you cannot conspire with your spouse.

C JANE and JOHN only.

D All three of them.

Question 2.4

TAYLOR is the licensee of the Masons Arms public house, which is wholly owned by a well-known major brewing company. He contacts his friend CROCKET, who makes a very potent real ale home brew. They agree to install a barrel of the real ale and sell it at the pub, contrary to the licence TAYLOR holds which allows him to sell only the brewery's beers.

Would TAYLOR and his friend be guilty of the offence of conspiracy, contrary to common law in these circumstances?

A Yes, but only if it can be shown that the customers were not aware that what they were drinking was not produced by the brewery.

B No, because TAYLOR's friend is not employed by the brewery and it takes at least two persons to conspire to commit the offence.

C Yes, but only if it can be shown that the company actually lost business as a result of TAYLOR and his friend's actions.

D Yes, both TAYLOR and his friend would be guilty of the offence in these circumstances.

Question 2.5

Constable HILL is standing in the forthcoming election for police federation representative. Having spoken to many of his colleagues Constable HILL is confident of election as most have indicated they will vote for him. However, to avoid disappointment he makes an agreement with Constable WITHERALL to ensure success. They agree to collect voting slips from a number of officers stating that there is a printing error and that another will be sent to them by the federation office. The officers take these forms and complete them in favour of Constable HILL, falsely signing the forms themselves. The result of the election was overwhelming and Constable HILL was elected achieving 90 per cent of the vote. In fact Constable HILL would have won the vote without submitting any of the voting slips that he submitted himself.

In these circumstances have the two officers committed an offence under common law of conspiracy to defraud?

A Yes, the officers have signed the forms dishonestly and in doing so have committed this offence.

B Yes, the officers have deprived their colleagues of their right to vote for who they want and in doing so have committed this offence.

C No, there is no statutory offence of 'vote rigging' and as the end result of their action is not an offence they have not committed this offence.

D No, their actions did not affect the outcome of the vote, and as no one was deprived of their right to be elected they have not committed this offence.

Question 2.6

The offence of vehicle interference is laid out in s. 9 of the Criminal Attempts Act 1981.

Which of the following must the prosecution prove to make the offence of vehicle interference complete?

A An intention to commit one of the further offences mentioned.
B An intention to commit any of the further offences mentioned.
C An interference only; no intention is needed.
D An interference along with evidence that the vehicle is a motor vehicle.

Question 2.7

YOUNG wishes to kill his wife who will not grant him a divorce, and looks for a contract killer. The police, however, are aware of his plan and send an undercover officer to meet him. YOUNG and the officer agree that for £2,000 the officer, posing as a contract killer, will shoot and kill YOUNG's wife. Naturally the officer has no intention of committing the murder.

In relation to conspiracy, which of the following is true?

A As an agreement has been reached to carry out an offence, this is a statutory conspiracy.
B As an agreement has been reached to carry out an offence, this is a common law conspiracy.
C As the officer will not carry out the murder, the offence of conspiracy is not made out.
D Although the officer will not carry out the murder, YOUNG is still guilty of conspiracy.

Question 2.8

EVANS tries to persuade SCHALK to distribute leaflets in the street. Both persons are aware that the leaflets may stir up racial hatred, and both know it is an offence to distribute these leaflets. EVANS only uses persuasion and does not pressurise or intimidate SCHALK. Although SCHALK took the leaflets, he did not distribute them, he burned them.

In relation to the common law offence of incitement, which of the following is true?

A EVANS has incited SCHALK even although he only used persuasion.

B EVANS has incited SCHALK as SCHALK took the leaflets from EVANS.

C EVANS has not incited SCHALK as no pressure was put on SCHALK.

D EVANS has not incited SCHALK as no offence was committed by SHALK.

Question 2.9

GILLIGAN is very short of cash and decides a robbery of the local post office is his only option. He gets hold of an imitation firearm, which he hides in his coat pocket; he then gets on a bus to the post office. He gets off the bus, and immediately loses his nerve and waits in the queue for another bus to go back home. He is about 10 metres from the entrance to the post office, but never draws his weapon.

At what point, if any, does GILLIGAN commit an offence of attempted robbery?

A When he decides he will commit the robbery.

B When he puts the gun in his pocket.

C When he gets off the bus outside the post office and waits.

D He does not commit an attempted robbery.

Question 2.10

THRUSH is an undercover officer working on a drugs operation. The police are carrying out an operation on GRIMES, a known drug dealer. THRUSH is authorised (proper authorities for this operation have been obtained) to purchase drugs from GRIMES. He approaches GRIMES who offers to sell him a wrap of amphetamine. THRUSH hands over the money and takes the drugs. During the transaction THRUSH asks GRIMES if he can supply a firearm for a robbery he is planning. GRIMES agrees to this and plans a later meeting.

In relation to THRUSH's request, which of the following is true?

A This is not entrapment as GRIMES is volunteering to get the firearms.

B This is not entrapment as the undercover operation has been authorised.

C This may be entrapment as THRUSH is no longer a passive observer.

D This is entrapment as THRUSH was not authorised by the operation to buy firearms.

Question 2.11

BOWLES was a carer for an elderly person, STANLEY. BOWLES believed that STANLEY was wealthy and set out to discover if he had made a will and who would inherit his estate when he died. Over a period of six months, BOWLES continually asked STANLEY questions in an attempt to gain this information, without success. Eventually, STANLEY became suspicious that BOWLES had been stealing items from his house and reported her to the police. The police arrested BOWLES and found the stolen items in her house, together with a will that she had written leaving STANLEY's entire estate to her. The will was dated six months previously and was unsigned. When interviewed, BOWLES admitted that she was only going to use it if she found out that STANLEY had no relatives to inherit his estate.

In these circumstances, would BOWLES commit the offence of attempting to make a false instrument, contrary to s. 1 of the Criminal Attempts Act 1981?

A Yes, when she actually wrote the will.

B No, as her intention to commit the offence was conditional on whether STANLEY had any other family.

C No, as she had not committed an act which was more than merely preparatory.

D Yes, when she attempted to find out details of STANLEY's family and whether or not he had made a will.

Question 2.12

MANNING was on holiday in Spain with his wife and while he was there, he became friendly with STUBBS. During a conversation one evening, MANNING told STUBBS that he was fed up with his wife and wished she were dead. STUBBS told MAN-NING that for a fee, he would kill his wife. The pair then discussed how this might happen and in the end they agreed that when they all returned to the UK, STUBBS would carry out the act. Unknown to them, their conversation was overheard by PAINTING, an off-duty police officer. Upon returning from holiday, PAINTING made a witness statement regarding the conversation to the local Crown Prosecution Service.

Could MANNING and STUBBS be prosecuted for an offence of conspiracy to commit murder in these circumstances?

A Yes, provided they return to this country to commit the substantive offence.

B Yes, whether or not they return to this country to commit the substantive offence.

C Yes, but only if the act of conspiracy would amount to an offence in Spain.

D No, a person may only be guilty of conspiring in this country to commit an offence abroad.

ANSWERS

Answer 2.1

Answer **D** — Incitement involves encouraging or pressurising someone to commit an offence. As can be seen the offence is complete when the person incited is 'encouraged' to commit the offence, and not just where 'pressurised'; answer C is therefore incorrect.

There is no requirement that the person incited actually goes on to commit the substantive offence or even that they form the intention to do so; answers A and B are therefore incorrect.

It is a necessary element of incitement, however, that the person incited be capable of committing the primary offence themselves as outlined by the Court of Appeal in *R v Whitehouse* [1977] QB 868 and *R v Pickford* [1994] 3 WLR 1022.

This principle was confirmed in a sexual offence case involving a boy under the age of 14 who could not have committed the primary offence because of an irrebuttable presumption of law that existed at the time (namely that a boy under the age of 14 was incapable of sexual intercourse) — *R v C* [2005] EWCA Crim 2827.

Crime, para. 1.3.2

Answer 2.2

Answer **C** — A charge under this section can be brought for agreements to commit indictable or summary offences (answer A is incorrect). However, the offence is only triable on indictment (answers B and D are incorrect).

Crime, para. 1.3.3.1

Answer 2.3

Answer **D** — One of the exclusions to conspiracies is that husband and wife cannot conspire, but this is when they agree together as the sole conspirators. If, however, a husband and wife conspire with a third person who is not a child under 10 or the intended victim, all three may be liable to conviction (*R v Chrastny* [1991] 1 WLR 1381 confirmed in *R v Lovick* [1993] Crim LR 890), and therefore answers B and C are incorrect. Conspiracy does occur even though the offence intended never occurs and therefore answer A is incorrect. Once the agreement is made the offence is complete.

Crime, para. 1.3.3.1

Answer 2.4

Answer **D** — The common law offence of conspiracy to defraud is expressly preserved by s. 5(2) of the Criminal Law Act 1977. It is defined in the leading case of *Scott* v *Metropolitan Police Commissioner* [1975] AC 819, where Viscount Dilhorne said:

> ... an agreement by two or more [persons] by dishonesty to deprive a person of something which is his or to which he is or would be or might be entitled [or] an agreement by two or more by dishonesty to injure some proprietary right of his suffices to constitute the offence ...
>
> ... it suffices if there is a dishonest agreement to expose the proposed victim to some form of economic risk or disadvantage to which he would not otherwise be exposed.

The situation in the question deprives the company of its right to sell its own product (see *R* v *Cooke* [1986] AC 909, where buffet car staff were selling their own sandwiches on British Rail trains). It is immaterial whether the company actually made a loss; because the company has been *exposed* to economic risk, therefore answer C is incorrect. Also, it is immaterial whether the customers realised that what they were drinking was not produced by the brewery, as the brewery is actually the loser in this scenario, and answer A is incorrect. Lastly, the offence is committed when the two people agree to deprive the company of profits — the fact that only one of them is employed by the brewery is not relevant, and answer B is incorrect.

Crime, para. 1.3.3.2

Answer 2.5

Answer **B** — Conspiracy to defraud involves:

> ... an agreement by two or more [persons] by dishonesty to deprive a person of something which is his or to which he is or would or might be entitled [or] an agreement by two or more by dishonesty to injure some proprietary right [of the victim] ...

There are two principal variants of this offence, although these are not mutually exclusive. The first is defined above in the leading case of *Scott* v *Metropolitan Police Commissioner* [1975] AC 819. There may or may not be an intent to deceive in such cases, and there may or may not be an intent to cause economic or financial loss to the proposed victim or victims, but it suffices if there is a dishonest agreement to expose the proposed victim to some form of economic risk or disadvantage to which he would not otherwise be exposed.

The second variant was also recognised in *Scott*, but has been more fully considered by the Privy Council in *Wai Yu-Tsang* v *The Queen* [1992] 1 AC 269. In this variant, there must be a dishonest agreement by two or more persons to 'defraud' another, by deceiving him into acting contrary to his duty.

Although the requirement for an agreement between at least two people is the same, this offence is broader than statutory conspiracy. There is no requirement to prove that the end result would amount to the commission of an offence, simply that it would result in depriving a person of something under the specified conditions or in injuring his/her proprietary right; answer C is therefore incorrect.

A good example of this offence can be found in *R v Hussain* [2005] EWCA Crim 1866 where the defendant pleaded guilty to conspiracy to defraud after a widespread abuse of the recently introduced postal voting system. In that case the defendant, an official Labour party candidate, collected uncompleted postal votes from households and completed them in his own favour. In that case it was shown that the end result was unlikely to have been affected by the defendant's actions, as it was likely he would have been elected in any case; however this has no effect on the commission of the offence of conspiracy to defraud. The offence is complete when an agreement is reached; answer D is therefore incorrect and is not limited to some dishonest *actus reus* like signing the forms fraudulently; answer A is therefore incorrect.

The *actus reus* of this offence is the agreement, the *mens rea* is the intent of the offender to defraud the victim (*R v Hollinshead* [1985] AC 975), and the dishonesty of the defendant as set out in *R v Ghosh* [1982] QB 1053.

Crime, para. 1.3.3.2

Answer 2.6

Answer **B** — This is a crime of specific intent, so you need to prove interference with a motor vehicle or trailer, and as such answer D is incorrect (note there is no definition of what interference is). You do, however, have to show an intention to commit theft of the vehicle/trailer, *or* theft from it *or* TADA (taking and driving away); therefore, C is incorrect. It is not necessary to show intention to commit any particular one of the further offences, and intention to commit any of them would suffice; therefore, answer A is incorrect.

Crime, para. 1.3.4.1

Answer 2.7

Answer **C** — A person cannot be guilty of conspiracy if the only other party to the supposed agreement intends to frustrate or sabotage it. As the officer clearly will frustrate the agreement, answers A and D are incorrect. This was considered by the House of Lords in *Yip Chieu-Chung* v *The Queen* [1995] 1 AC 111, where N, the appellant's only fellow conspirator in a plan to smuggle heroin out of Hong Kong, was an undercover agent working with the knowledge of the authorities. The House of Lords held that if N's purpose had been to prevent the heroin being smuggled, no indictable conspiracy would have existed. Their Lordships said:

> The crime of conspiracy requires an agreement between two or more persons to commit an unlawful act with the intention of carrying it out. It is the intention to carry out the crime that constitutes the necessary *mens rea* for the offence....[A]n undercover agent who has no intention of committing the crime lacks the necessary *mens rea* to be a conspirator.

Conspiracy requires an agreement which will amount to or involve the commission of an offence. Where no such offence is likely, the offence is not made out. Common law conspiracy involves conspiracy to defraud only and therefore B is incorrect.

Crime, paras 1.3.3.1, 1.3.6.3

Answer 2.8

Answer **A** — A person may incite another to do an act by threatening or by pressure, as well as by persuasion, therefore answer C is incorrect. Incitement can be committed even if the incited person refuses to act, or does not commit the actual offence incited, therefore answer D is incorrect. The offence is complete when the inciter uses persuasion in an attempt to incite another to commit the offence. It is irrelevant that SCHALK took the leaflets; the offence was already committed before this action took place, and answer B is incorrect.

Crime, para. 1.3.2

Answer 2.9

Answer **D** — He does not commit the offence in these circumstances. In *R* v *Gullefer* [1990] 1 WLR 1063, Lord Lane CJ stated that the crucial question was whether the accused had 'embarked upon the crime proper', but that it was not necessary that the accused should have reached a 'point of no return' in respect of the full offence. So at what point in time are the actions of GILLIGAN more than merely preparatory? Certainly his actions involved in getting to the post office were merely preparatory: the forming of the intent (answer A is incorrect); putting the weapon in his pocket (answer B is incorrect). The only time his actions may be more than preparatory is when he is outside the post office. However, intent is the essence of any crime of attempt under the Criminal Attempts Act 1981. The prosecution must ordinarily prove that the accused acted with a specific intent to commit the particular crime attempted. GILLIGAN loses the intent when he steps off the bus, therefore answer C is incorrect. And although he is in proximity to the post office, without the requisite intent he cannot commit attempted robbery.

Crime, para. 1.3.4

Answer 2.10

Answer **C** — The question of police entrapment is an emotive one. Where the line was drawn between legitimate police activity in undercover operations and the police acting as *agents provocateurs* was sometimes fuzzy. The House of Lords laid down the legal position in this issue in *R v Loosely; Attorney General's Reference (No. 3) of 2000* [2001] 1 WLR 2060, where it was held, *inter alia*:

> A useful guide is to consider whether the police did no more than present the defendant with an unexceptional opportunity to commit a crime. The yardstick for the purposes of this test is, in general, whether the police conduct preceding the commission of the offence was no more than might have been expected from others in the circumstances.

Was the officer enticing the accused to commit an offence he would not otherwise have committed? He was committing the offence of drug dealing, and was not entrapped there, but the officer goes beyond being a passive observer when he asks about the firearm. In *Loosely*, their Lordships stated:

> The police must act in good faith. Having reasonable grounds for suspicion is one way good faith may be established. It is not normally considered a legitimate use of police power to provide people not suspected of being engaged in any criminal activity with the opportunity to commit crimes. The principle is that the police should prevent and detect crime, not create it.

So the fact the operation was authorised does not negate entrapment by an individual officer (answer A is incorrect); nor does the fact that the accused seems keen to carry out the officer's request (answer B is incorrect). What is also clear is that simply going beyond what is authorised is not necessarily entrapment; it depends on the officer's action — answer D is therefore incorrect. This area of law has guidelines set down, but ultimately it is for the judge to decide if actions amount to entrapment, and whether such entrapment should lead to a stay of proceedings or not, which is why answer C states 'may be entrapment'.

Crime, para. 1.3.6.1

Answer 2.11

Answer **C** — The scenario is based on the case of *R v Bowles* [2004] EWCA Crim 1608, a case in which the defendant had been convicted of offences of dishonesty against his neighbour. The neighbour's will left her estate to charity, but following his arrest police officers found a 'new' will, fully complete except for a signature. The defendant and his wife were named as the main beneficiaries. Although the defendant's son had been overheard making reference to the fact that he was going to inherit the house, the new will had been drafted over six months earlier and there was no evidence of any steps to execute it, nor any evidence that it had ever been used. The Court of Appeal held that the making of the will was no more than merely preparatory and the defendant's conviction for attempting to make a false instrument was quashed. Answers A and D are therefore incorrect.

A defendant's intention *may* be conditional, that is, he/she may only intend to steal from a house if something worth stealing is later found inside. Answer B is therefore incorrect. The conditional nature of this intention will not generally prevent the charge of attempt being brought and the defendant's intentions will be judged *on the facts as he/she believed them to be.* However, careful drafting of the charge may be required in cases where there is doubt as to the precise extent of the defendant's knowledge at the time he/she was caught (see *R v Husseyn* (1978) 67 Cr App R 131).

Crime, para. 1.3.4

Answer 2.12

Answer **B** — Under s. 1(1) of the Criminal Law Act 1977, a person is guilty of conspiracy if he/she agrees with any other person(s) that a course of conduct will be pursued which, if the agreement is carried out in accordance with their intentions, either —

(a) will necessarily amount to or involve the commission of any offence or offences by one or more of the parties to the agreement; or

(b) would do so but for the existence of facts which render the commission of the offence or any of the offences impossible.

Offences may sometimes be tried in our country even though they were committed abroad. If the object of a conspiracy would amount to an offence under the jurisdiction of the relevant country *and* of England and Wales, the conspiracy may be tried under the Criminal Law Act 1977, s. 1A. In addition, it was held in *R v DPP ex parte Manning* [1999] QB 980 that if people conspire abroad to commit offences in

England and Wales they may, under certain circumstances, be indicted under English and Welsh law even if none of the conspirators enters the jurisdiction to do so. Answers A and D are therefore incorrect.

It would not be necessary to consider whether the act of conspiracy would amount to an offence in Spain, because the intention would be to prosecute the offence in this country. Answer C is therefore incorrect.

Crime, para. 1.3.3.1

3 | General Defences

STUDY PREPARATION

There is little point in collecting evidence, arresting where necessary and charging a person only to find that they raise a specific or general defence at trial — a defence which the investigating officer could have addressed in interview or when taking witness statements. For this reason alone it is important to know what defences may exist in relation to certain offences. Similarly, as the police are under a duty to investigate fully and impartially, it is important to know what defences may be available to a defendant.

A number of offences have specific defences contained in the relevant statute, and these are (not surprisingly) called statutory defences. In addition, there are a number of 'general defences', some of which are statutory and others existing at common law. It is helpful to divide general defences into two categories:

1. Those which involve a denial of the basic requirements of *mens rea* and voluntary conduct (the defences of mistake and automatism are best regarded in this way).
2. Those which do not deny these basic requirements but which rely on other circumstances of excuse or justification, as in the defences of duress and self-defence.

The integration of the Human Rights Act 1998 and the European Convention on Human Rights into English law is also important in this area of study.

QUESTIONS

Question 3.1

SMITH is driving his motor vehicle at 70 mph in the outside lane of a motorway, with his window open. A bee flies in through the window and, as he fears being stung, SMITH tries to kill it with his newspaper. Momentarily distracted, he fails to notice the vehicle in front has slowed and he runs into the back of it. Police investigate and he is reported for an offence of careless driving.

In these circumstances could SMITH use the defence of automatism?

A Yes, his actions were not voluntary or willed.

B Yes, as he cannot be held liable for his actions as he lost control.

C No, although a reflex action it would not amount to automatism.

D Yes, provided he could not have foreseen the bee flying in.

Question 3.2

O'GRADY and GLADSTONE had been drinking in a nightclub all night. GLADSTONE claimed he was an SAS soldier. They left together to go to O'GRADY's flat. The next morning, O'GRADY made an emergency call saying that he had been out all night and had returned to find an unknown man dead in his home; this male was GLADSTONE; near the deceased's body was a sledgehammer. Under GLADSTONE's body was found a stick, some five feet in length, which belonged to O'GRADY and which he had fashioned to resemble a samurai sword. O'GRADY stated that if he had killed GLADSTONE, he might have acted in self-defence in that GLADSTONE might have attacked him with the stick, and he might have used the sledgehammer to defend himself. O'GRADY stated that his drunken state might have led him to believe, albeit mistakenly, that the deceased was an SAS soldier attacking him with a sword.

In relation to the claim of a mistaken belief of self defence induced by voluntary intoxication which of the following is correct?

A This defence could only apply where the charge was murder given the specific intent required for such a charge.

B This defence could only apply where the charge was manslaughter as this is a basic intent offence.

C This defence will always be available in homicide offences, but only so far as sentencing is concerned.

D This defence will not apply as a defendant cannot rely on a mistake induced by their own voluntary intoxication.

Question 3.3

THOMPSON has been charged with an offence of murder for killing her husband during a domestic dispute and wishes to claim the defence of insanity. She claims that at the time of committing the offence she was suffering from 'a disease of the mind'.

Who must decide the question of whether THOMPSON was suffering from 'a disease of the mind'?

A The judge, as it is a question of law.
B The jury, as it is a question of fact.
C Any doctor, as it is a question of medical opinion.
D A psychologist, as it is a question of specialist medical opinion.

Question 3.4

DUGGAN, a law lecturer, has been stopped by Constable GARDNER to check his driving documents. During the stop, Constable GARDNER believes she can smell alcohol and requests a breath test. DUGGAN takes the test, which is positive, and the officer arrests him. DUGGAN says 'that took longer than 40 seconds to go red, your arrest is unlawful' and tries to leave. The officer stops him and DUGGAN punches her. DUGGAN is charged with an offence of assault with intent to resist arrest. DUGGAN says in interview that he honestly, but mistakenly, believed that the arrest was unlawful.

Considering this offence only, could DUGGAN avail himself of the defence of mistake?

A Yes, provided his belief was genuinely held.
B Yes, as what he did was 'inadvertent'.
C Yes, provided he could show his actions were 'reasonable'.
D No, in these circumstances the defence would not be available.

Question 3.5

NEWMAN, aged 15, has been bullied at school by a gang of youths. The gang are well known for shoplifting in the lunch hour in the local shops. One evening, while his parents were out, NEWMAN received a phone call from one of the gang members, stating that the gang wanted him to steal a pair of trainers from a sports shop on the way into school. The caller stated that if he did not comply, he would be severely beaten the next day in school by members of the gang. NEWMAN was very scared and the next day tried to steal a pair of trainers.

In relation to any possible defence that NEWMAN might have, which of the following is correct?

A NEWMAN would not be able to rely on the defence of duress in these circumstances, as it applies to threats of death only.

B Provided NEWMAN held a genuine belief that he would be seriously injured if he did not commit the crime, he would have a defence of duress in these circumstances.

C NEWMAN would be able to rely on the defence of duress in these circumstances, as a threat was made. It is immaterial whether he believed the threat or not.

D NEWMAN would not be able to rely on the defence of duress in these circumstances, as the threat was not immediate.

Question 3.6

BREWSTER is a member of a gang who, to his knowledge, use loaded firearms to carry out robberies on sub-post offices. The other gang members discuss a forthcoming robbery, and BREWSTER is aware of the plan. During the robbery another member of the gang shoots and kills the sub-post master and they all make good their escape. BREWSTER is later caught and charged with robbery. BREWSTER wishes to use the defence of duress. He claims his wife was threatened at gunpoint after he tried to pull out of the robbery, and he took part only because he feared for his wife's life.

Will BREWSTER be allowed to use duress as a defence?

A Yes, as his wife's life was threatened.

B No, the defence will not be available in these circumstances.

C No, the threat must have been against BREWSTER's life.

D Yes, provided the person who issued the threat was the one who shot the sub-post master.

Question 3.7

BEVAN parks his car whilst he goes into a restaurant for a meal. He meets a friend and ends up drinking more than he had intended. Believing he would be over the legal limit for driving, BEVAN returns to his car to collect his laptop computer, fully intending to get a taxi. There is now a large gang near his car. The gang are very aggressive and BEVAN fears for his personal safety. As they charge at him, he jumps into his car and drives away. He stops about half a mile further down the road, and parks the car, intending to take a taxi. However, a police officer sees BEVAN and breathalyses him, the result of which is positive. BEVAN is charged with a drink driving offence.

Will BEVAN have a defence to this offence?

A Yes, he could claim duress.

B Yes, he could claim duress of circumstances.

C No, there is no defence to drink driving offences.

D No, general defences apply to criminal offences only.

Question 3.8

Doctor TAYLOR keeps a quantity of cannabis at her surgery, the sole purpose of which is to dispense to sufferers of various illnesses that caused severe pain to the patient. The doctor had found that cannabis was more effective than any other proprietary medicine that was available, and that use of cannabis was the only way to reduce the severe pain that her patients were in. This was the only defence she had raised when questioned by the police about her actions.

Will the doctor have a defence of possession of controlled drugs with the intention of supplying them using a general defence?

A Yes, provided the doctor could justify that she was conducting medical research.

B Yes, provided the doctor reasonably believed that what she was doing was a medical necessity.

C No, in these circumstances the doctor will have no general defence to possession with intent to supply.

D No, because she did not raise her actions as a 'human rights' issue; in that case she may well have had a defence.

Question 3.9

Constable EAST is on the tactical firearms unit, and has been called to a hostage situation. Unfortunately, the incident ends when Constable EAST fatally shoots RICHARDS, who was the assailant.

In relation to the lawfulness of EAST's use of lethal force, what test will be applied?

A That he had an honestly held belief that it was necessary.

B That such force was reasonable in the circumstances.

C That such force was no more than absolutely necessary.

D That such force was necessary to protect the life of another.

Question 3.10

HOOD is a keen archer and has permission from THOMAS to use his land for practice. THOMAS even tells him that there is a scarecrow in a field that he can fire at. HOOD takes his high-powered bow and fires an arrow at the scarecrow from 200 metres. Being a good shot he hits the scarecrow, but is surprised when the scarecrow falls over. He goes to investigate and is horrified to find he has just shot a rambler who had stopped to check his map.

Could HOOD use the defence of mistake if he was charged with murder?

A   No, he was under a positive obligation to check what he was aiming at.

B   No, he should have checked with the landowner if there was a public footpath.

C   Yes, as he had the landowner's authority, the landowner is vicariously liable.

D   Yes, as he did not have the requisite *mens rea*.

Question 3.11

The police were called to a domestic disturbance at the home of BUCKLEY and his wife DENISE. On their arrival, officers were confronted by BUCKLEY, a six foot two male, of heavy build, and DENISE, who was five foot two and of slim build. DENISE had suffered a deep cut to the back of her head and claimed it was caused by BUCKLEY, who had pushed her against a wall. BUCKLEY claimed that he was acting in self-defence, as DENISE had attacked him with a vase and that he had only pushed her away with the open palm of his hand. BUCKLEY was arrested for assault by the officers.

Which of the following statements is correct in relation to what factors the court might take into consideration if BUCKLEY were to claim self-defence?

A   The court would not take into account the relative sizes of BUCKLEY and DENISE; the issue is whether BUCKLEY held a genuine belief that the force was reasonable in the circumstances.

B   In the circumstances, the court would have expected BUCKLEY to retreat when he perceived the threat from DENISE.

C   The court would not take into account the gender of BUCKLEY and DENISE; the issue is whether BUCKLEY held a genuine belief that the force was reasonable in the circumstances.

D   The court may take into account both the relative sizes of BUCKLEY and DENISE, and the gender difference.

Question 3.12

BRENDOUNE was found in possession of a shotgun and on the way to commit a burglary. When he was arrested and interviewed, however, he stated that his wife was being held captive by an armed gang who threatened to kill her if he did not commit the burglary. He also stated that it was his idea and not the gang's that he should take the shotgun; his intention was to use it to resist arrest and he felt his wife's life was in danger.

Considering that BRENDOUNE has committed an offence contrary to the Firearms Act 1968, s. 18 (carrying a firearm or imitation firearm with intent to resist arrest), will he be able to claim the defence of duress?

A Yes, but only if he can show that the intention to resist arrest was as a result of duress.

B Yes, in these circumstances duress is available as a defence, as this was the reason he took the shotgun.

C No, duress is not available as he was only asked to carry out a burglary, the firearms offence was his idea.

D No, the defence of duress is not available if the threat is made against a third party, unless they are present at the time of the offence.

Question 3.13

In relation to the defence of duress of circumstances, the person accused of an offence must have acted in a certain way.

In relation to what caused the person to behave as they did which of the following is correct?

A The person must be impelled to behave as they did because they themselves actually feared a criminal act being committed.

B The person must be impelled to behave as they did because a reasonable person in those circumstances would fear a criminal act being committed.

C The person must be impelled to behave as they did because a criminal act was actually being committed there and then.

D The person must be impelled to behave as they did because they perceived a threat that in itself would not amount to a criminal act.

Question 3.14

WADE and FRENCH have been jointly charged with an offence of aggravated burglary. It is alleged by the prosecution that during the burglary of a dwelling house,

WADE and FRENCH assaulted and seriously injured the elderly occupant. WADE is aged 10 and FRENCH is aged 14.

Which of the following statements is correct, in relation to criminal liability of both defendants?

A Because of their ages, the prosecution *may* be asked by the court to adduce evidence to show that both knew that what they had done was seriously wrong where challenged by the defence to do so.

B Both WADE and FRENCH are criminally liable for the offence as charged, irrespective of their ages.

C Because of his age, FRENCH is criminally liable; however, the prosecution *may* be asked by the court to adduce evidence that to show that WADE knew that what she had done was seriously wrong.

D Because of their ages, the prosecution *will always* be asked by the court to adduce evidence that to show that both knew that what they had done was seriously wrong.

ANSWERS

Answer 3.1

Answer **C** — The defence of automatism applies only where the loss of control is *total*, which makes answers A and B incorrect. The example in the Manual is where a swarm of bees flew into a car causing the driver to lose control. In the circumstances of the question, a temporary loss of concentration caused by the driver trying to swat the bee could not be seen to be a total loss of control, as is required for the defence to succeed; it is a *voluntary* action by the driver to swat the bee, not a loss of his self-control. This defence does not involve any foresight to certain risks, so answer D is also wrong.

Crime, para. 1.4.2

Answer 3.2

Answer **D** — The principal restriction imposed on defences based on intoxication is that voluntary intoxication can only give rise to a defence to crimes of specific rather than basic intent as the courts have also accepted that a defendant is still capable of forming basic intent even when completely inebriated (see *DPP* v *Majewski* [1977] AC 443).

This is further complicated where the defence used relates to a mistaken belief. Although the principle that an accused who mistakenly believes he is being attacked may be able to rely on the defence of self-defence this does not apply where the accused's mistake was due to voluntary intoxication (*R* v *O'Grady* [1987] QB 995). Although the actual conviction in *O'Grady* was for manslaughter (a basic intent offence), the Court of Appeal seemed clear in the view that an intoxicated mistake could not be relied upon even in relation to a crime of specific intent such as murder. This view was further endorsed by the Court of Appeal in *R* v *Hatton* (2006) 1 Cr App R 16; the court held that on the proper application of the law of precedence, the general principle that was the reason for the court's decision in *O'Grady* was not to be regarded as mere *obiter dicta* (remarks of a judge which are not necessary to reaching a decision, but are made as comments, illustrations or thoughts) so far as the law of murder was concerned. Accordingly, the court was bound by the decision, and there were no grounds to argue that the judge should have directed the jury to consider whether the defendant's drunkenness might have led him to make a mistake as to the severity of any attack to which he might have been subjected by the deceased.

The specific defence raised in this scenario cannot be raised in a case of manslaughter or murder; answers A and B are therefore incorrect. Although in manslaughter cases mitigation is allowed in sentencing, a conviction for murder leaves a judge no discretion in sentencing a defendant; answer C is therefore incorrect.

Crime, paras 1.4.3.1, 1.4.8.2

Answer 3.3

Answer **A** — The question of whether a person is suffering from 'a disease of the mind' is a question of law, and therefore the judge must decide and not the jury. Therefore, answer B is incorrect. It is not a question of medical opinion, specialist or not (*R* v *Sullivan* [1984] AC 156), making answers C and D incorrect.

Crime, para. 1.4.4

Answer 3.4

Answer **D** — The defence of mistake will only be used to negate the *mens rea* of the offence charged. The question is 'did the defendant assault the officer to resist arrest'? The answer is 'yes' and DUGGAN could not claim to have been 'mistaken' as to whether the officer had a power of arrest or not (*R* v *Lee*, *The Times*, 24 October 2002). However, the defence might have been available had he mistakenly believed that the officer was not really a police officer. In the case of *Blackburn* v *Bowering* [1994] 1 WLR 1324, Sir Thomas Bingham said (at p. 1329): 'the important qualification [is] that the mistake must be one of fact (particularly as to the victim's capacity) and not a mistake of law as to the authority of the person acting in that capacity'. So as answers A, B and C all refer to DUGGAN's belief/actions, they are incorrect as the *mens rea* is clear.

Crime, para. 1.4.5

Answer 3.5

Answer **D** — Generally speaking, where a person is threatened with death or serious physical injury unless he or she carries out a criminal act, he or she may use the defence of duress. Note that this includes a threat of serious injury, not just death, therefore answer A is incorrect (see *R* v *Graham* [1982] 1 WLR 294). There are, however, caveats to this general use of duress. One of these caveats is that the threatened injury must be anticipated at or near the time of the offence (i.e. not some time in the distant future). As the threat was for the following day NEWMAN could not use the defence, and answers B and C are both incorrect.

Crime, para. 1.4.6

Answer 3.6

Answer **B** — The defence of duress is not available to a person who joins a violent gang, knowing that they might put pressure on him to commit an offence (*R v Sharp* [1987] QB 853). The question follows the broad outline of Sharp. A threat of death or serious harm to a partner may allow the defence of duress (as in *R v Ortiz* (1986) 83 Cr App R 173 where threats to the accused's wife or family were considered to be sufficient). Answers A, C and D all refer to some sort of threat or other, and are made incorrect by the fact that BREWSTER knew that pressure may be applied to him.

Crime, para. 1.4.6

Answer 3.7

Answer **B** — Duress of circumstances is available in traffic cases, so answers C and D are incorrect. BEVAN has to show that his actions were reasonable (*R v Martin* [1989] 1 All ER 652). Here his actions could be regarded as 'reasonable', as he feared for his safety. The fact he stopped soon after supports this claim, and the defence has succeeded in similar circumstances (*DPP v Bell* [1992] RTR 335). Contrast this with *DPP v Jones* [1990] RTR 33, where a similar defence failed because the accused drove all the way home, without even checking whether he was still being chased. The facts of this question would not support a defence of 'duress' as no threat has been made, which is a necessary component of that defence, which makes answer A incorrect.

Crime, para. 1.4.7

Answer 3.8

Answer **C** — The Court of Appeal has considered this specific issue in *R v Quayle and Others* [2005] 1 WLR 3642, specifically whether a defence of medical necessity could be left to the jury in relation to offences of cultivation, production, possession, possession with intent to supply or importation of cannabis allegedly committed for the purpose of alleviating severe pain.

In *Quayle* the Attorney General made a reference in respect of a defence of 'medical necessity', concerned as to whether or not the defence of necessity was available in respect of drugs offences such as possession of cannabis with intent to supply where the defendant intended to supply the drug for the purpose of alleviating pain from a pre-existing illness (such as multiple sclerosis).

It was also argued that the common law defence of necessity should be expanded to prevent or remove any inconsistency with statutory legislation such as the European Convention on Human Rights. Dismissing the appeals, the Court held that necessary 'medical use' claimed on an individual basis was in conflict with the purpose and effect of the legislative scheme (in particular the Misuse of Drugs Act 1971 and the relevant Regulations); answer B is therefore incorrect. No such use was permitted under the legislation, even on doctor's prescription, except in the context of ongoing trials for medical research purposes. In this scenario the doctor could not attempt to justify that her actions were for research; for this defence to work evidence of proper research and trials would have to exist; answer A is therefore incorrect.

The legislative scheme did not permit unqualified individuals to prescribe cannabis to themselves as patients or to assume the role of a doctor by obtaining, prescribing and supplying it to other 'patients'. Neither can a defendant rely on the same defence by presenting it as a 'human rights' issue (*R* v *Altham* [2006] EWCA Crim 7); answer D is therefore incorrect.

For the defence of necessity of circumstances to be potentially available, there has to be 'extraneous circumstances capable of objective scrutiny by judge and jury' (per *R* v *Hasan* [2005] UKHL 22) and the legal defences of duress by threats and 'necessity' should be confined to cases where there was an imminent danger of physical injury and pain.

Crime, paras 1.4.6, 1.4.7

Answer 3.9

Answer **C** — The test applied under s. 3(1) of the Criminal Law Act 1967 — such force as is reasonable in the circumstances — has been superseded, as far as lethal force is concerned, by Article 2 of the European Convention on Human Rights. Under the Convention the test for such force is now no more than 'absolutely necessary'; in addition it must be strictly proportionate to the legitimate purpose being pursued. Anything other than this strict test will not be enough, making answers A, B and D incorrect.

Crime, para. 1.4.8.1

Answer 3.10

Answer **D** — The defences of mistake and inadvertence consist of a denial of the *mens rea* of the particular crime charged. The *mens rea* for murder is the intention to kill or cause grievous bodily harm. So in relation to this defence you can generalise that wherever an offence requires individual awareness of a particular element, a genuine mistake that such an element is absent will be a defence. The logic of this rule is irrefutable as applied to crimes requiring intention. If a man believes he is shooting at an inanimate object such as a scarecrow, he cannot at the same time by that very act intend to kill. Consider the offence of handling stolen goods, where particular information is required. A person who believes that the goods he buys are not stolen cannot at the same time know (or even believe) that the goods are stolen — the two states of mind are logically inconsistent with one another. However, some offences require some degree of foresight or awareness of risk, and these offences create problems for those wishing to avail themselves of this defence; they would have to show ruling out of any risk of the prohibited consequences (see *Chief Constable of Avon and Somerset Constabulary* v *Shimmen* (1986) 84 Cr App R 7). Here the accused claimed to have ruled out the risk of causing damage to a window when he aimed a martial-art-style kick in its direction, basing his view on his faith in his own prowess as an exponent of the Korean art of self-defence. In other words, he claimed to believe that no damage would result from his action (the subsequent shattering of the window revealing this belief to be a sadly mistaken one). So HOOD, if charged with murder, would not have to show foresight of what he was aiming at, or whether there might be a person as opposed to an inanimate object in the field, where he was to use this defence; answers A and B are therefore incorrect. And even with the landowner's permission, were HOOD to have the requisite *mens rea* for murder, this defence would not be available; answer C is therefore incorrect.

Crime, para. 1.4.5

Answer 3.11

Answer **D** — In deciding whether or not the force used by a defendant was reasonable in the circumstances, the courts may take into account matters such as the relative height, build and strength of the defendant and the person against whom the force was used and the injuries caused. The court may also take into account the gender of the parties (see *R (on the application of Buckley)* v *DPP* [2004] EWHC 2533). In this case, the court also found that even an open-handed push could amount to unreasonable force in the circumstances. Answers A and C are therefore incorrect.

There is no requirement to let the believed attacker 'strike the first blow' (see *Beckford* v *The Queen* [1988] AC 130) *or* for the person defending themselves to retreat (see *R* v *Bird* [1985] 1 WLR 816). A 'pre-emptive' strike may be justified by the circumstances. Answer B is therefore incorrect.

Crime, para. 1.4.8.2

Answer 3.12

Answer **A** — Firstly let's consider the offence under the Firearms Act 1968, s. 18 which states:

(1) It is an offence for a person to have with him a firearm or imitation firearm with intent to commit an indictable offence, or to resist arrest or prevent the arrest of another, in either case while he has a firearm or imitation firearm with him.

It is important to note that the offence asked of him is different from the offence he stands accused of; this does not mean *per se* that he cannot use the defence of duress. However, where applicable intent is a fundamental element of an offence, the accused must show that he/she had, or could only have formed that intent by reason of that duress. Without showing that the only compelling factor in the formation of the relevant intent is duress, then the defence will fail (*R* v *Fisher* [2004] EWCA Crim 1190); answer C is therefore incorrect. Note the relevant intent here is that of resisting arrest, not possession of the shotgun; therefore answer B is incorrect.

The question is whether the threat has to be directed at the accused or whether threats to third parties, especially close relatives, can suffice. There seems to be consensus amongst legal commentators on this point and certainly in principle threats to third parties should be capable of constituting duress. Even the bravest man may be prepared to risk his own neck whilst baulking at subjecting his loved ones to serious peril. Indeed there is Australian authority recognising threats to the accused's common-law wife, and in *R* v *Ortiz* (1986) 83 Cr App R 173 threats to the accused's wife or family appear to have been considered to be sufficient; answer D is therefore incorrect.

Crime, para. 1.4.6

Answer 3.13

Answer **D** — As well as cases where a person receives a direct threat in order to make them commit an offence, there may be times when circumstances leave the defendant no real alternative. In *R v Cairns* [1992] 2 Cr App R 137 the court held that the jury must ask two questions in relation to this 'necessary action':

- Was he (or might he have been) impelled to act as he did because, as a result of what he reasonably believed, he had good cause to fear he would suffer death or serious injury if he did not do so?
- If so, would a sober person of reasonable firmness and sharing the same characteristics, have responded to the situation in the way that he did?

If each question were answered with a 'yes', the defence would be made out.

In the case of *R v Jones (Margaret) & Others* [2004] EWCA 1981, the Court of Appeal considered whether a case of necessity/duress of circumstances could be made out for a person who used force in the honestly held belief that in doing so he was protecting the property of others abroad from damage that would be caused by the executive's lawful exercise of the prerogative power to wage war. The Court accepted that that the defence of necessity was available if a defendant could show that he acted to prevent an act of greater evil but there was no requirement that the act of greater evil should be unlawful. This effectively means that a person can act in duress of circumstances where the threat (or perceived threat) does not amount to a criminal act. Therefore answers A, B and C are incorrect as they relate to criminal acts or perceptions of criminal acts.

Crime, para. 1.4.7

Answer 3.14

Answer **B** — Before the Crime and Disorder Act 1998, children under 14 years of age were subject to a rebuttable presumption at common law to be 'incapable of evil' or *doli incapax*. The presumption of *doli incapax* in relation to children who were aged 10 or over but who had not yet reached 14 years of age was *rebuttable*. This meant that the prosecution could adduce evidence to show that the child defendant knew that what he/she had done was seriously wrong. If the evidence was accepted, the courts would regard that presumption as having been rebutted and the child defendant could be tried in much the same way as an adult. Some concern as to how appropriate such a presumption was in modern society led the House of Lords in *C (a Minor) v DPP* [1995] 2 WLR 383 to declare the rule to be outdated but adding that it was up to Parliament to change it. Section 34 of the Crime and Disorder Act 1998 did exactly that and abolished this second, rebuttable form of the presumption of *doli incapax*, effectively lowering the age of criminal responsibility to 10 years of age.

In relation to children under 10 years of age that presumption was, and still is irrebuttable. Consequently, no evidence to the contrary will be entertained by a court and children under 10 cannot be convicted of a criminal offence.

Since both defendants are over 10, they are both criminally liable for their actions and answers A, C and D are incorrect.

Crime, para. 1.4.10

4 | Homicide

STUDY PREPARATION

This chapter contains the law relating to some of the most serious charges a person can face. Although these offences are still relatively rare and are usually dealt with by specialist investigators, it is important to know the constituent elements — particularly as it is often more a case of good fortune which prevents people involved in assaults and woundings from facing these more serious charges. In addition to the offences themselves, the chapter deals extensively with the special defences associated with an indictment for murder. It is worth noting that there are three different types of manslaughter offences, and it is worth learning the differences between them.

QUESTIONS

Question 4.1

WILSON has had a stormy relationship with his girlfriend, who is now seven months' pregnant. One night in a fit of rage he hits her so hard she falls and bangs her head on the wall. She is taken into hospital and goes into early labour. The child is born alive but dies three days later. When interviewed by police, WILSON admits that his intention was only to cause serious injury to the mother.

Which is the most appropriate charge relating to the death of the baby?

A Murder.

B Manslaughter.

C Grievous bodily harm owing to transferred malice of intention.

D No offence in relation to the death of the baby.

Question 4.2

There are three special defences open to a person charged with an offence of murder.

Should they be successful, what is the legal effect of these defences?
A They would allow an acquittal.
B They would allow a conviction of manslaughter.
C They would allow a partly reduced sentence.
D They would allow a greatly reduced sentence.

Question 4.3

BURKE suffers from a congenital degenerative brain disease, but is still fully competent. He is concerned that in the future he may be denied artificial nutrition and hydration (ANH) that would be required to keep him alive. This fear is based on a directive from the General Medical Council to practitioners that 'Where death is not imminent, it usually will be appropriate to provide artificial nutrition or hydration. However, circumstances may arise where you judge that a patient's condition is so severe, the prognosis so poor, that providing artificial nutrition or hydration may cause suffering or to be too burdensome in relation to the possible benefits'.

Considering possible homicide offences and the right to life contained in Article 2 of the European Convention on Human Rights which of the following is correct?
A Specifically in BURKE's case at any time in the future withholding ANH could lead to a charge of murder against the doctor withholding it.
B Any case where ANH is withheld could lead to a charge of murder against the doctor withholding it.
C Withholding treatment that might not be in the patient's best interest has been held to be incompatible with Article 2 of the European Convention on Human Rights.
D A patient can demand any treatment that would prolong their life and this right is afforded by Article 2 of the European Convention on Human Rights.

Question 4.4

AMIR, BROOKES and SHARP decide they want to end their lives and form a written agreement. They intend to shoot each other in a game of Russian roulette which involves loading a gun with four bullets, one of which is a blank. They load the revolver and spin the chamber. AMIR fatally shoots BROOKES in the head, and then SHARP fatally shoots AMIR in the head. SHARP then turns the gun on himself but the next bullet is blank. Thankful to be alive, SHARP panics and runs from the scene.

In relation to suicide pacts, if SHARP is to use this as a 'special defence' to murder, which of the following must be shown?

A Only that such a pact existed at the time SHARP shot AMIR.

B That a pact existed and that SHARP intended to shoot himself next.

C That a written agreement existed between AMIR and SHARP.

D That a written agreement existed between all the parties.

Question 4.5

HOLLY and his common law wife had been to the local pub where they had been drinking heavily and arguing. HOLLY returned to their flat where he chopped wood with an axe and drank more lager. The common law wife was still in a public house drinking. When she returned to the flat she told HOLLY she had just had sex with another man. HOLLY picked up the axe, intending to leave the flat and chop some more wood, when his common law wife said, 'You haven't got the guts'. He struck her seven or eight times with the axe, killing her, and is charged with murder.

HOLLY wishes to use 'provocation' as a defence; for the purposes of the defence of provocation by what standard should he be judged?

A He will be judged on whether a 'reasonable' or ordinary person would have lost his self-control in these circumstances.

B He will be judged on whether a 'reasonable' or ordinary person, who was also drunk, would have lost his self-control in these circumstances.

C He will be judged on his own particular circumstances, particularly that he was drunk.

D He will be judged on his own particular circumstances, but not the fact that he was drunk.

Question 4.6

NEAL and MENDEZ were hunting fanatics. While hunting in the local woods, NEAL thought he would play a joke on MENDEZ. NEAL pointed his rifle at MENDEZ, believing there were no bullets in the chamber, and pulled the trigger. However, he had not checked the gun properly and MENDEZ was hit by a bullet in the chest. MENDEZ was taken to the local hospital, where he subsequently died.

In relation to any homicide offences committed by NEAL, which of the following is correct?

A NEAL is guilty of murder in these circumstances, as he was reckless in his actions.

B NEAL is guilty of manslaughter in these circumstances, as he was reckless in his actions.

C NEAL is not guilty of manslaughter by an unlawful act, as he had no intention to injure MENDEZ.

D NEAL is guilty of manslaughter in these circumstances, as he was negligent in relation to his gun.

Question 4.7

BRANDRICK has been charged with an offence of attempted murder.

What is the *mens rea* required to support such a charge?

A Intention to kill the victim.

B Intention to cause grievous bodily harm.

C Intention either to kill the victim or to cause grievous bodily harm.

D Recklessness as to whether the victim dies or not.

Question 4.8

DEEN is an ardent and devout Muslim who created audiotapes for others to listen to. These were of an inflammatory nature and urged Muslims to fight and kill, among others, Jews, Christians, Americans, Hindus and other unbelievers. He encouraged his listeners to kill. He encouraged them to wage Jihad against the enemies of Islam as he deemed them to be. When questioned by police, DEEN stated that when he spoke of killing, he was speaking only of killing in self-defence.

Is this solicitation to murder?

A No, as he did not personally encourage, only through the tapes.

B No, as there was no specific threat against someone.

C No, as he has not coerced people to murder for him.

D Yes, as he has sought to solicit and encourage murder.

Question 4.9

WILLOUGHBY owned a taxi firm which was failing financially. WILLOUGHBY owned the building which contained the firm's office and decided to set fire to the building to claim from the insurance company. WILLOUGHBY enlisted the help of a friend, DYTHAM, who had no connection with the company, and one evening they went to the building with cans of petrol and matches. WILLOUGHBY spread the petrol around the inside of the premises and lit a fire, while DYTHAM stood near the door as the lookout. Unfortunately, when the petrol ignited there was an explosion which killed DYTHAM and injured WILLOUGHBY. WILLOUGHBY was subsequently charged with manslaughter.

In relation to WILLOUGHBY's liability for the offence of manslaughter, which of the following statements is correct?

A WILLOUGHBY would be guilty of manslaughter by unlawful act in these circumstances.

B WILLOUGHBY would not be guilty of manslaughter, as DYTHAM actually assisted with the crime.

C WILLOUGHBY would be guilty of manslaughter by gross negligence in these circumstances.

D WILLOUGHBY would not be guilty of manslaughter; the intention was to commit arson, not to injure DYTHAM.

Question 4.10

LAMB has been charged with an offence of murder and is due to appear in court. LAMB intends pleading not guilty to murder and will ask the court to accept a plea of guilty to the offence of manslaughter on the grounds of diminished responsibility.

Which of the following is correct, in respect of the 'impairment of responsibility' that LAMB must have suffered, in order to succeed with this approach?

A The impairment suffered must have been substantial and must also have been the sole cause of LAMB's actions in committing the manslaughter.

B The mental impairment must have been substantial, and it must be shown that it contributed in some way to LAMB's actions in committing the manslaughter.

C The mental impairment need not be substantial, provided it contributed in some way to LAMB's actions in committing the manslaughter.

D The mental impairment need not be substantial, provided it can be shown that it was the sole cause of LAMB's actions in committing the manslaughter.

ANSWERS

Answer 4.1

Answer **B** — The House of Lords decided in *Attorney General's Reference* (*No. 3 of 1994*) [1998] AC 245 that the unborn child is not simply a part of its mother but that they are distinct organisms. They also held, however, that the doctrine of transferred malice does not fully apply, and therefore answer C is incorrect. An intention to inflict grievous bodily harm on the mother cannot attract liability for murder in respect of the subsequent death of the child (answer A is incorrect), although there will still be a liability for the death of the child, answer D is therefore incorrect. If the intention was to kill the mother and to cause the child to die after having been born alive, there may be an offence of murder but we are not told this in the facts given.

Crime, para. 1.5.2

Answer 4.2

Answer **B** — There are three special defences to murder and all three are governed by the Homicide Act 1957. All three are partial defences, reducing the offence from murder to manslaughter rather than leading to an outright acquittal. Answer A is therefore incorrect. These defences are needed principally because the mandatory life sentence for murder does not leave any discretion to the judge in sentencing whereby he or she can take account of factors such as provocation, as would normally be the case with lesser offences where the sentence is not fixed by law. Consequently, answers C and D are incorrect.

Crime, para. 1.5.3

Answer 4.3

Answer **C** — A particularly emotive issue, that I'm sure the courts find as difficult to deal with as any other legislative issue that comes before them.

Considering first the right to life enshrined in Article 2 of the European Convention on Human Rights, in particular, the positive obligation imposed on a State to protect the lives of its citizens. Article 2 creates both a duty on the State not to take life and also a positive duty to protect the lives of individuals (see *X* v *United*

Kingdom (Application 7154/75) (1978) 14 DR 31); this has been examined legislatively and in *NHS Trust A* v *M* [2001] 2 WLR 942 the Court of Appeal held that the taking of a responsible clinical decision to withhold treatment that was not in the patient's best interests met the State's positive obligation under Article 2; answer C is therefore incorrect.

This is not to say, however, that where treatment is withheld a doctor cannot be held accountable, and with criminal consequences. In *R (On the Application of Burke)* v *General Medical Council* [2005] 3 WLR 1132, where a patient's express wish to continue with life-prolonging treatment was considered, the Court of Appeal clarified the situation. In that case the Court considered the situation where artificial nutrition and hydration (ANH) would be required for a patient until he died of natural causes.

Among its other findings, the Court held that Article 2 would plainly be violated if a doctor were to bring about the death of a competent patient by withdrawing life-prolonging treatment contrary to that patient's wishes. In addition, where a competent patient indicated a wish to be kept alive by the provision of ANH any doctor who deliberately brought that patient's life to an end by discontinuing the supply of ANH would be guilty of murder. In the circumstances of this scenario the patient was competent and that would be the deciding factor; clearly where a patient was not competent to make a decision, and where there were sound clinical decisions for withholding treatment, the Courts have indicated that this would not amount to criminal actions by the doctor; answer B is therefore incorrect.

The decision in *Burke* was decided on its own facts, and particularly on the provision of ANH. This cannot be seen as a mandate for patients to demand any treatment to prolong their life, as doctors still have to consider patients' autonomy versus their 'best interests'; for this reason answer D is therefore incorrect.

The complex legal issues in the 'right to life' debate will no doubt continue to be considered in the courts, where decisions come under very close scrutiny by both sides involved actively in that debate.

Crime, para. 1.5.1.1

Answer 4.4

Answer **B** — A suicide pact is formed when a common agreement is made between two or more persons, having for its object the death of all of them. It does not have to be written, but does have to be an agreement between all involved. A suicide pact allows for a conviction of manslaughter, and not murder, where the accused was acting in pursuance of such a pact.

The defendant must show that a suicide pact had been made, *and* he or she had the intention of dying at the time the killing took place. (Therefore, answers C and D are incorrect.)

This means that the existence of the pact is not enough (answer A is therefore incorrect) — at the time of the killing there must also be an intention of dying.

Crime, para. 1.5.3.3

Answer 4.5

Answer **A** — The defence of provocation is outlined in the Homicide Act 1957, s. 3 which states:

> Where on a charge of murder there is evidence on which a jury can find that the person charged was provoked (whether by things done or by things said or by both together) to lose his self-control, the question whether the provocation was enough to make a reasonable man do as he did shall be left to be determined by the jury; and in determining that question the jury shall take into account everything both done and said according to the effect which, in their opinion, it would have on a reasonable man.

The main questions to be considered are:

- Was the defendant actually provoked?
- Might a reasonable person have acted as the defendant did under the same circumstances?

Most problematic is what the 'reasonable person' means, and here the decisions in the courts are at the least confusing!

The House of Lords considered this area and the competing authorities in *R v Smith (Morgan James)* [2001] 1 AC 146. That decision attempted to set out the components of the 'reasonable person' test and the factors that a jury may take into account when assessing whether or not provocation can be claimed by the defendant — factors such as those peculiar to the defendant (e.g. suffering from 'battered woman syndrome' or a personality disorder. *Morgan Smith* was a controversial decision and many legal experts disagreed with it; however even that decision, which gave some guidance, has effectively been overturned. The Privy Council (which exercised through its Judicial Committee is the provision of a final Court of Appeal for a number of Commonwealth countries who have chosen to retain it) heard an appeal from Jersey (*Attorney General for Jersey* v *Holley* [2005] 2 AC 580), the House of Lords sitting as Lords of Appeal in Ordinary decided the question of the reasonable person very differently from their decision in *Morgan Smith*.

The standard that a person will be judged on for this defence now is whether having regard to the actual provocation and the jurors' view of its gravity, a person having ordinary powers of self-control would have done what the defendant did. The effect of the alcohol having no effect to this particular defence, answers B, C and D are therefore incorrect.

The only consideration is that as this is a case from Jersey how binding is it on English law; however as Professor A.J. Ashworth put it in Crim LR 2005, Dec, 966–971

Is *Holley* binding on English courts? There may be a purist strain of argument to the effect that it is not, since it concerns another legal system (that of Jersey). However, the reality is that nine Lords of Appeal in Ordinary sat in this case, and that for practical purposes it was intended to be equivalent of a sitting of the House of Lords. It is likely that anyone attempting to argue that *Morgan Smith* is still good law in England and Wales would receive short shrift ...

Crime, para. 1.5.3.2

Answer 4.6

Answer **C** — Like most offences, homicide requires that the defendant had the required *mens rea* for the relevant 'unlawful act', which for homicide offences would lead to the death of a victim. If the defendant did not have that *mens rea*, the offence of manslaughter will not be made out and therefore answers A, B and D are incorrect. In the case of *R v Lamb* [1967] 2 QB 981, the defendant pretended to fire a revolver at his friend. Although the defendant believed that the weapon would not fire, the chamber containing a bullet moved round to the firing pin and the defendant's friend was killed. As Lamb did not have the *mens rea* required for an assault his conviction for manslaughter was quashed.

Crime, para. 1.5.4.1

Answer 4.7

Answer **A** — According to CPS Charging Standards, para. 10.3, 'unlike murder, which requires an intention to kill or cause grievous bodily harm, attempted murder requires evidence of an intention to kill alone'. Thus an intention to kill is the required *mens rea* for this offence and therefore answers B, C and D are incorrect.

Crime, para. 1.5.2, App.1.2

Answer 4.8

Answer **D** — There is no requirement that the solicitation be made in person (answer A is incorrect), nor that there be a particular person under threat (answer B is incorrect). The scope of the behaviour sufficient to constitute the offence was classically identified as follows in *R v Most* (1881) 7 QBD 244 *per* Huddleston B, at p. 258:

> The largest words possible have been used — 'solicit' — that is defined to be, to importune, to entreat, to implore, to ask, to attempt to try to obtain: 'encourage', which is to intimate, to incite to anything, to give courage to, to inspirit, to embolden, to raise confidence, to make confident, 'persuade' which is to bring any particular opinion, to influence by argument or expostulation, to inculcate by argument: 'endeavour' and then, as if there might be some class of cases that would not come within those words, the remarkable words are used, 'or shall propose to', that is say, make merely a bare proposition, an offer for consideration.

This wide interpretation means that coercion is not required; therefore answer C is incorrect. The facts of this question mirror that of *R v El-Faisal* [2004] EWCA Crim 343, where the Court of Appeal upheld the conviction of El-Faisal for solicitation to murder through the production of tapes that urged Muslims to kill unbelievers.

Crime, para. 1.5.7

Answer 4.9

Answer **A** — The circumstances in the question are similar to those in *R v Willoughby* [2004] EWCA Crim 3365, where the court examined a case of arson on the defendant's own public house. In the first instance, the Court of Appeal found that provided the defendant's conduct (intentionally starting the fire) had been the cause of the death, the jury were bound to convict the defendant of manslaughter. Answer D is therefore incorrect. The defendant in *Willoughby* was found guilty, even though the victim in the case was also the accomplice in similar circumstances to this question, therefore answer B is incorrect.

The Court of Appeal examined whether or not the defendant should have been found guilty of manslaughter by gross negligence. The Court held that it was entirely unnecessary to have recourse to manslaughter by gross negligence in this case as it was a straightforward case of manslaughter by unlawful act. Answer C is therefore incorrect. However, it was also held even though the offence of manslaughter by gross negligence was unsuitable in this case, there may be occasions where the defendant could be guilty of manslaughter via either avenue.

Crime, para. 1.5.4.2

Answer 4.10

Answer **B** — Under s. 2 of the Homicide Act 1957, a defendant may be acquitted of murder, but be liable instead for manslaughter, if the person is able to show the court that he/she was suffering from such abnormality of mind (whether arising from a condition of arrested or retarded development of mind or any inherent causes or induced by disease or injury) as *substantially* impaired his/her mental responsibility for his/her acts or omissions in doing or being a party to the killing. The mental impairment suffered must be substantial and minor lapses of lucidity will not be enough. Answers C and D are therefore incorrect.

In the case of *R v Dietschmann* [2003] 1 AC 1209, the House of Lords accepted that a mental abnormality caused by a grief reaction to the recent death of an aunt with whom the defendant had had a physical relationship could suffice. In that case their Lordships went on to hold that there is no requirement to show that the 'abnormality of mind' was the sole cause of the defendant's acts in committing the killing. Answers A and D are therefore incorrect.

Crime, para. 1.5.3.1

5 | Misuse of Drugs

STUDY PREPARATION

Offences relating to the misuse of drugs require a sound knowledge both of the elements of the offences and the case law that supports them. You should also understand the elements of the statutory defences that apply, and how they affect the case in question. This chapter also covers the rather complicated power to enter, search and seize granted by s. 23 of the Misuse of Drugs Act 1971, and it is well worth taking your time over this section (if you've read it you'll know what I mean!). In addition to the more usual controlled drugs, this chapter also includes the law relating to intoxicating substances.

QUESTIONS

Question 5.1

Constable FOSTER asks your advice regarding the offence of supplying articles for administration or preparing controlled drugs (under s. 9A of the Misuse of Drugs Act 1971). She has received information regarding HAINING, who is supplying hypodermic syringes to drug users who are using them to inject themselves with heroin. Constable FOSTER asks you what action she can take.

In relation to the above offence, which of the following is correct?

A Constable FOSTER can apply for a search warrant under the 1971 Act.

B Constable FOSTER can arrest HAINING for committing the offence, where the officer feels it is necessary to arrest the person in question.

C Constable FOSTER cannot arrest HAINING as this is NOT an indictable offence, proceed by summons only.

D The offence is not complete; hypodermic syringes are not included in this offence.

Question 5.2

GOSS has a bottle of vitamin tablets in her handbag. Unknown to her, her son had put three Ecstasy tablets in the bottle that morning. Before leaving the house GOSS checks that she has the bottle in her handbag.

Which of the following is correct?

A GOSS is in possession of a controlled drug, but may not be committing an offence.

B GOSS is in possession of a controlled drug and is committing an offence.

C GOSS is not in possession of a controlled drug as she did not put them in the bottle.

D GOSS is not in possession of a controlled drug as she has no knowledge of what they are.

Question 5.3

Detective Constable JONES is a member of the National Crime Squad. She has been involved in an undercover operation in relation to drug trafficking. STEER is a major drug dealer and has asked JONES to help in the supply of cocaine. JONES has provisionally agreed to this to maintain her cover. In fact JONES has no intention of illegally supplying drugs, and the arrest of STEER is considered as necessary.

In relation to incitement under s. 19 of the Misuse of Drugs Act 1971, which of the following is correct?

A The offence is complete when STEER asks JONES to supply the drugs.

B As JONES has no intention of supplying the drugs, the offence is not complete.

C The offence would be complete only if JONES actually supplied the drugs.

D The offence is complete only if STEER receives the drugs, and supplying is complete.

Question 5.4

PATEL is a self-employed chemist and her partner, NEWMAN, confessed to her that he was a heroin addict, although not registered as such. PATEL was shocked by the news, but agreed to help NEWMAN break his addiction. PATEL took some methadone from her storeroom, and gave it to NEWMAN.

In relation to PATEL's actions, which of the following is incorrect?

A PATEL has committed no offence in these circumstances, as she had lawful possession of the drug.

B Even though PATEL would normally be entitled to lawfully possess a controlled drug, she has committed an offence by supplying it to NEWMAN.

C PATEL has committed an offence in these circumstances.

D PATEL has committed an offence from the time she took the drug from the surgery intending to supply it to NEWMAN.

Question 5.5

MEREDITH found a bag containing white powder in her son's bedroom, which she believed was cocaine. MEREDITH took the powder, intending to hand it in to the police. However, as a leader of the local youth club, MEREDITH decided to keep the drugs to show other youth workers, so they will be able to recognise the drug should they find any.

Would MEREDITH be able to claim a statutory defence to the offence of possession of a controlled drug, under s. 5(4) of the Misuse of Drugs Act 1971?

A Yes, providing it was her intent to destroy the drugs when she took possession of them to prevent her son from committing an offence.

B No, the defence would only apply if she took possession of the drugs and subsequently destroyed them.

C No, the defence would only apply if she took possession of the drugs and subsequently delivered them to a person lawfully entitled to possess them.

D No, the defence would only apply if she took possession of the drugs and either destroyed them or delivered them to a person lawfully entitled to possess them.

Question 5.6

HAMMOND is a customs officer working undercover. She is part of an on-going operation regarding drug supply at the 'Green Man' public house. The officer goes to the pub to make a test purchase, and is shown several wraps containing white powder by HAYES, a suspected drug dealer. HAYES states that the wraps contain amphetamine and will cost £30 per wrap. In fact the wraps contain baking powder, a fact of which HAYES is unaware. The transaction takes place.

Which of the following offences, if any, does HAYES commit?

A Possession of a controlled drug.

B Possession with intent to supply a controlled drug.

C Offering to supply a controlled drug.

D Supplying a controlled drug.

Question 5.7

BARTON and HOLLOWAY are business partners. HOLLOWAY uses her factory for the production of Ecstasy. BARTON ensures that the premises are not disturbed by providing 24-hour security in the factory, and also provides transportation to the factory of the raw goods required for the production of Ecstasy. BARTON neither visits the factory, nor has any direct contact with the security or transportation, but is aware of what happens at the factory. HOLLOWAY never visits the factory either.

Who, if anyone, is guilty of unlawful production of a controlled drug under s. 4 of the Misuse of Drugs Act 1971?

A BARTON.

B HOLLOWAY.

C Both of them.

D Neither of them.

Question 5.8

BOOKER has long been suspected by the police of being involved in the supply of controlled drugs and a warrant has been obtained to search his premises. The police go to BOOKER's house and, as they enter, BOOKER takes various papers and shreds them. BOOKER is unsure whether they are evidence or not, but is not willing to take a chance. These papers actually amounted to the only real evidence proving BOOKER's involvement in the supply of controlled drugs.

Has BOOKER committed an offence of obstruction under s. 23(4) of the Misuse of Drugs Act 1971?

A Yes, he was reckless as to whether the papers were evidence or not.

B Yes, he has obstructed the officers by destroying the evidence.

C No, as obstruction only applies to deliberate, physical obstruction of the officers themselves.

D No, as obstruction only applies to stop/searches in relation to drugs.

Question 5.9

Police suspect that DAWLISH is using her premises to allow persons to enter and smoke cannabis. Her neighbours have complained that the noise is continual, both day and night, and have asked the police if they can do something to stop the occurrence of the disorder associated with persons entering and leaving DAWLISH's house.

In relation to using the premises for the unlawful use, production or supply of a controlled drug which of the following is correct?

A A police officer not below the rank of superintendent may authorise the issue of a closure notice in respect of the premises in these circumstances.

B A police officer not below the rank of inspector may authorise the issue of a closure notice in respect of the premises in these circumstances.

C A closure notice can only be applied for by the local authority in these circumstances.

D No closure notice may be authorised in these circumstances.

Question 5.10

GORDON has a controlled drug in his pocket, which he intends to supply to someone else. Seeing a police officer in the distance, he hands the drugs to his friend, MEREDITH, and says 'hold on to these for me and I will give you £20'. MEREDITH agrees and takes possession of the drugs. The officer walks past them and MEREDITH hands the drugs back to GORDON and collects his £20.

In relation to the controlled drugs, which offence(s) has MEREDITH committed?

A Possession only.

B Supply only.

C Possession or supplying only.

D Possession or supplying or possession with intent to supply.

Question 5.11

GOULD is 16 years old and works on Saturdays in his father's shop. He sells a bottle of solvent to his school friend whom he knows is 16 years old.

Under s. 1 of the Intoxicating Substances (Supply) Act 1985 (supply of an intoxicating substance), which of the following is correct in relation to the defences available to GOULD?

A GOULD has a defence owing to his age only.

B GOULD has a defence as he was acting in the course of a business.

C GOULD has a defence owing to his age and the fact that he was acting in the course of a business.

D GOULD has no defence.

Question 5.12

BUCKLEY and HARRIS are both drug addicts and bought a quantity of heroin together, which BUCKLEY actually carried back to a house. At the house, BUCKLEY divided the heroin equally and gave a share to HARRIS. Unfortunately, HARRIS had been drinking all day and fell asleep. BUCKLEY then injected HARRIS with her own drugs while she was asleep.

At what point, if at all, does BUCKLEY commit the offence of supplying a controlled drug, under s. 4(3)(a) of the Misuse of Drugs Act 1971?

A When BUCKLEY divided the heroin and gave it to HARRIS.

B Only when BUCKLEY injected HARRIS with the heroin.

C On both occasions, when BUCKLEY divided the heroin and gave it to HARRIS and later when HARRIS was injected with the heroin.

D The offence is not committed at all, because the heroin was jointly purchased by BUCKLEY and HARRIS.

Question 5.13

Travel restriction orders made under the Criminal Justice and Police Act 2001 restrict the travel of convicted drug traffickers.

For how long a period does this travel restriction order last?

A Two years.

B Four years.

C Ten years.

D Unlimited period; no set maximum.

Question 5.14

MAY was the sole tenant and occupier of a flat, which was raided by the police. They found MAY, along with seven others, and a number of items used for the smoking of drugs. They also found a quantity of cannabis resin. MAY admits he had given permission for drug smoking to take place. During the search of the premises the police could detect no smell of cannabis. MAY was charged with allowing the offence of permitting the smoking of cannabis, cannabis resin or prepared opium on premises under s. 8 of the Misuse of Drugs Act 1971.

Is MAY guilty of this offence?

A Not guilty, as he was not the owner of the premises.

B Not guilty, as there was no evidence actual smoking took place.

C Guilty, as there was cannabis and drugs paraphernalia in the premises.

D Guilty, as he admits that he gave permission for drug smoking.

Question 5.15

Police are considering a closure notice under s. 1 of the Anti-social Behaviour Act 2003, with regard to a club which has been used in connection with supplying Class A drugs.

In relation to the officer who can authorise this, and how long this individual can go back in relation to the club's activities (the officer is considering issuing the order today), which of the following is true?

A An officer of at least the rank of assistant chief constable (ACC) can authorise, and can consider the use of the club over the past month.

B An officer of at least the rank of superintendent can authorise, and can consider the use of the club over the past month.

C An officer of at least the rank of ACC can authorise, and can consider the use of the club over the past three months.

D An officer of at least the rank of superintendent can authorise, and can consider the use of the club over the past three months.

Question 5.16

Police officers are executing a warrant under s. 23 of the Misuse of Drugs Act 1971 at a house. The warrant allows for the searching of persons as well as the premises. In the house are several people, including a gas meter reader, who states he was there to read the meter. The police wish to search him, but he wants to go and read other meters.

Which of the following is true?

A They can search the meter reader, but only with his permission.

B They can search the meter reader, and can require him to remain for that purpose.

C They cannot search the meter reader, only the occupier of the premises.

D They cannot search him, only the occupier and persons present with his permission.

Question 5.17

Section 4 of the Anti-social Behaviour Act 2003 creates offences in relation to premises subject to a closure notice or order.

Which of the following would amount to one of these offences?

A Entering the premises.

B Obstructing a constable without reasonable excuse.

C Obstructing an authorised person acting within their powers.

D Remaining on the premises.

Question 5.18

MILLIGAN was approached by GIVENS and asked to deliver a package to a nearby address. GIVENS gave MILLIGAN £200 for taking the package. MILLIGAN was very drunk at the time he was asked to take the package and did not realise that he had been given so much money. He takes the package but is stopped by police officers who have had GIVENS, a known drug dealer, under surveillance. The package is found to contain a very large quantity of a Class A drugs and MILLIGAN is charged with possession of, and possession with intent to supply, a Class A drug.

Consider MILLIGAN's use of the defence under s. 28(2) of the Misuse of Drugs Act 1971 (lack of knowledge of some alleged fact) due to the fact he was drunk and he had no 'reason to suspect' what he was doing.

Which of the following is correct?

A The defence could be used for possession of the drugs, but not for the intention to supply.

B The defence could *not* be used for either charge as 'reason to suspect' is a factual test and not subject to individual peculiarities.

C The defence could be used for either charge as 'reason to suspect' is subject to individual peculiarities and is not a factual test.

D The defence could be used for intention to supply but not for mere possession of the drugs.

Question 5.19

McGREGOR is walking down the street with his friend who is known to deal in drugs, but McGREGOR has no connections with illegal drugs. McGREGOR's friend sees a uniformed police officer walking towards them, and slips a bag containing several Ecstasy tablets into McGREGOR's jacket pocket, although she is unaware the officer saw what happened and decided to carry out a search on both persons. The officer finds the Ecstasy on McGREGOR and makes an arrest. McGREGOR denies that he even knew the drugs were there.

Taking into account only the term 'possession' in relation to possession of a controlled drug, which of the following is correct?

A To prove 'possession' you only have to show that the accused had physical possession of the drug.

B To prove 'possession' you only have to show that the accused had physical possession of the drug and knowledge that they were in fact a controlled drug.

C To prove 'possession' you only have to show that the accused knew he had possession of something, and that in fact that 'something' was a controlled drug.

D To prove 'possession' you only have to show that the accused knew he had possession of something, and suspicion that 'something' was a controlled drug.

ANSWERS

Answer 5.1

Answer **D** — This offence deals with the supplying of or offering to supply articles for use for preparing or administering controlled drugs. The offence is designed to address the provision of drug 'kits'. It specifically does not include hypodermic syringes, or parts of them (s. 9A(2)). The administration for which the articles are intended must be 'unlawful'. As the offence has not been committed, there is no action that the officer can take to either search or bring HAINING before justice, and therefore answers A, B and C are incorrect. The offence would be arrestable as s. 24 of the Police and Criminal Evidence Act 1984 is substituted by s. 110 of the Serious Organised Crime and Police Act 2005; but only where the officer deems it necessary to arrest where one of the criteria laid out in subsection (5) is met.

Crime, para. 1.6.7.8

Answer 5.2

Answer **A** — Common law outlines possession as physical control plus knowledge of the presence of the drugs. This becomes problematical where the person in possession claims not to realise what they possessed. In these cases you need to show that the person had physical control of the container together with knowledge that it contained something. GOSS knew she had a container and that it contained tablets (answers C and D are therefore incorrect). This simply means that GOSS was in possession of controlled drugs, not that she was committing an offence under the 1971 Act. It is clear from various case authorities that the basic elements are that a person 'knows' that they are in possession of something which is in fact a controlled substance. As answer C states that she is committing an offence for simply possessing the drugs, it is incorrect. She may commit an offence, as outlined in answer A; however, she could avail herself of the statutory defences available.

Crime, paras 1.6.5.1, 1.6.5.2, 1.6.5.3

Answer 5.3

Answer **A** — The definition of this offence under s. 19 of the Misuse of Drugs Act 1971 is 'for a person to incite. . .another to commit [an offence under this Act]'. This clearly covers all sections, not just supplying.

Although the offence of incitement exists for most other offences generally, the 1971 Act makes a specific offence of inciting another to commit an offence under its provisions.

On the arguments in *DPP* v *Armstrong* [2000] Crim LR 379, it would seem that a person inciting an undercover police officer may commit an offence under this section even though there was no possibility of the officer actually being induced to commit the offence, and therefore answer B is incorrect. As the offence is committed at the time the incitement is made and is not conditional on either the supply or receipt of the controlled drugs, answers C and D are incorrect.

Crime, para. 1.6.7.18

Answer 5.4

Answer **A** — Section 5 of the Misuse of Drugs Act 1971 states:

(3) Subject to section 28 of this Act, it is an offence for a person to have a controlled drug in his possession, whether lawfully or not, with intent to supply it to another in contravention of section 4(1) of this Act.

It is important to note that the lawfulness or otherwise of the possession is irrelevant; what matters here is the lawfulness of the intended supply. If a vet, or a police officer or some other person is in lawful possession of a controlled drug but they intend to supply it unlawfully to another, this offence will be made out.

This is a crime of specific intent and the intention to supply would have to be proven, as it is in the question. Consequently, PATEL commits an offence, making answers B, C and D actually correct in law. The question, though, asks you what is incorrect, and therefore answer A is actually the correct answer.

Crime, para. 1.6.7.6

Answer 5.5

Answer **D** — Defences are provided by s. 5(4) of the Misuse of Drugs Act 1971, which states:

In any proceedings for an offence under subsection (2) above in which it is proved that the accused had a controlled drug in his possession, it shall be a defence for him to prove —

(a) that, knowing or suspecting it to be a controlled drug he took possession of it for the purpose of preventing another from committing or continuing to commit an offence in connection with that drug and that as soon as possible after taking possession of it he took all such steps as were reasonably open to him to destroy the drug or to deliver it into the custody of a person lawfully entitled to take custody of it;

(b) that, knowing or suspecting it to be a controlled drug he took possession of it for the purpose of delivering it into the custody of a person lawfully entitled to take custody of it and that as soon as possible after taking possession of it he took all such steps as were reasonably open to him to deliver it into the custody of such a person.

It can be seen from the above that once MEREDITH had taken possession of the drugs, she would then be expected *either* to destroy them *or* deliver them to a person lawfully entitled to possess them — answers B and C are incorrect, because the defence is available to a person who does either of these things.

The issue of intent under s. 5(4)(b) above was examined in the case of *R* v *Dempsey and Dempsey* [1986] 82 Cr App R 291. In this case it was held that the defendant must prove that it was his/her *sole* intention at the time of taking possession of the drug to deliver it to a person lawfully entitled to possess it. However, even though it was MEREDITH's intent to hand the drugs in to the police when she actually took possession of the drugs, she later changed her mind and did not do so. From the point that she changed her mind, she was in unlawful possession of the drugs and would not be able to rely on the defence provided by s. 5(4) above. Answer A is therefore incorrect.

Crime, para. 1.6.6.1

Answer 5.6

Answer **C** — For the offences of possession, possession with intent to supply and supply, the prosecution would need to prove that the substance in question is in fact a controlled drug. Answers A, B and D are therefore incorrect. For the offence of offering to supply under s. 4(3)(c) of the 1971 Act, it does not matter whether the accused had a controlled drug in his or her possession or had easy access to a controlled drug.

Crime, para. 1.6.7.2

Answer 5.7

Answer **C** — The meaning of 'produce' and 'concerned in production' is defined by s. 37 of the Misuse of Drugs Act 1971, which states:

(1) ...'produce', where the reference is to producing a controlled drug, means producing it by manufacture, cultivation or any other method, and 'production' has a corresponding meaning; ...

Being concerned in production requires the accused to take an identifiable role in the production. Both BARTON and HOLLOWAY take an identifiable role in the production in that, although they never visit the premises, they have guilty knowledge of its function and, but for their actions, the production may not take place. This makes option C the only possible correct answer.

Crime, para. 1.6.7.1

Answer 5.8

Answer **B** — This offence is complete where the person obstructs someone carrying out stop/search procedures and also executing a warrant, and therefore answer D is incorrect. In *R* v *Forde* (1985) 81 Cr App R 19, it was held that a person only committed this offence if the obstruction was intentional, that is to say the act viewed objectively, through the eyes of a bystander, did obstruct the constable's search, and viewed subjectively, that is to say through the eyes of the accused himself, was intended so to obstruct. BOOKER knew he was intentionally obstructing the officers and, even though he was unsure of the outcome, recklessness does not apply (answer A is incorrect). Section 23(4)(b) of the Misuse of Drugs Act 1971 states that the offence includes a person who 'conceals from a person acting in the exercise of his powers under subsection (1) above any such books, documents ...'. So, as books and documents are included, answer C is incorrect.

Crime, para. 1.6.8.2

Answer 5.9

Answer **D** — Section 1 of the Anti-social Behaviour Act 2003 states:

This section applies to premises if a police officer not below the rank of superintendent (the authorising officer) has reasonable grounds for believing —
(a) that at any time during the relevant period the premises have been used in connection with the unlawful use, production or supply of a Class A controlled drug, and
(b) that the use of the premises is associated with the occurrence of disorder or serious nuisance to members of the public.

As can be seen closure notices only apply to circumstances surrounding the unlawful use, production or supply of a Class A controlled drug, and as cannabis is not

Class A in these circumstances a closure notice cannot be authorised; answers A, B and C are therefore incorrect.

Although in relation to the drug usage it is the police who authorise closure notices this must be done in consultation with the local authority (s. 1(2)(a)); there is also a general power for local authorities to make a closure order in relation to noise and nuisance being caused in connection with the use of premises under s. 40 of the 2003 Act.

Crime, para. 1.6.7.12

Answer 5.10

Answer **D** — In its simplest form, where one person hands over a controlled drug to another, there can be said to be a supply. Where a person leaves a controlled drug with another for safekeeping, the situation is trickier. Fortunately, the House of Lords have given direction in this area in two cases: *R v Maginnis* [1987] AC 303 and *R v Dempsey and Dempsey* (1986) 82 Cr App R 291. The outcome of these cases is that if the person looking after the drugs for another is in some way benefiting from that activity, then the return of those drugs to the depositor will amount to 'supplying' and the offences supplying or possession with intent to supply will be applicable as well as simple possession. None of these offences need stand alone in the circumstances outlined in the question, and therefore answers A, B and C are incorrect.

Crime, para. 1.6.7.3

Answer 5.11

Answer **D** — Section 1 of the Intoxicating Substances (Supply) Act 1985 defines the defence in subsection (2) as:

> in proceedings against any person for an offence under subsection (1) above it is a defence for him to show that at the time he made the supply or offer he was under the age of 18 and was acting otherwise than in the course or furtherance of a business.

So on the one hand GOULD does have a defence in that he is 16; but this does not stand alone as the statute says 'under the age of 18 *and*' — that 'and' makes answer A incorrect. The second part of the subsection concerns 'acting otherwise than in the course or furtherance of a business' and as GOULD was acting in the course of or in furtherance of a business, he is not afforded this defence and answers B and C are incorrect.

Crime, para. 1.6.9

Answer 5.12

Answer **A** — It is an offence under s. 4(3)(a) of the Misuse of Drugs Act 1971 to supply a controlled drug to another. It has been held that dividing up controlled drugs which have been jointly purchased *will* amount to 'supplying' (*R* v *Buckley* (1979) 69 Cr App R 371).

Further, injecting another with his/her own controlled drug has been held *not* to amount to 'supplying' in a case where the defendant assisted pushing down the plunger of a syringe that the other person was already using. Parker CJ's comments in that case suggest that simply injecting another person with their own drug would not amount to 'supplying' (*R* v *Harris* [1968] 1 WLR 769). It may, however, amount to an offence of 'poisoning' under s. 23 of the Offences Against the Person Act 1861.

Answers B, C and D are therefore incorrect.

Crime, paras 1.6.7.2, 1.6.7.3

Answer 5.13

Answer **D** — The introduction of the Criminal Justice and Police Act 2001, ss. 33–37, allows any criminal court (but effectively, given the sentencing restriction, this means the Crown Court) to impose a travel restriction order on an offender who is convicted of a drug trafficking offence. The offender has to have been sentenced by that court to a term of imprisonment for four years or more (s. 33(1)). The effect of the order is to restrict the offender's freedom to leave the United Kingdom for a period specified by the court, and it may require delivery up of his passport. The minimum duration of a travel restriction order is two years, starting from the date of the offender's release from custody. There is no maximum period prescribed in the legislation, therefore answers A, B and C are incorrect. The court must always consider whether such an order should be made and must give reasons where it does not consider such an order to be appropriate (s. 33(2)).

Crime, para. 1.6.8.3

Answer 5.14

Answer **B** — The Misuse of Drugs Act 1971, s. 8 states:

> A person commits an offence if, being the occupier or concerned in the management of any premises, he knowingly permits or suffers any of the following activities to take place on those premises, that is to say:

(a) producing or attempting to produce a controlled drug in contravention of section 4(1) of this Act;

(b) supplying or attempting to supply a controlled drug to another in contravention of section 4(1) of this Act, or offering to supply a controlled drug to another in contravention of section 4(1);

(c) preparing opium for smoking;

(d) smoking cannabis, cannabis resin or prepared opium.

As can be seen, it applies to occupiers and not just owners; answer A is therefore incorrect. It does, however, require that it was necessary to establish that the activity of smoking had taken place and not merely that the permission had been given (*R* v *August, The Times*, 15 December 2003); answer D is therefore incorrect. It is also not sufficient that the drugs and paraphernalia were present — it seems the police may have timed their raid a bit too soon as no smoking had taken place — answer C is therefore incorrect.

Crime, para. 1.6.7.10

Answer 5.15

Answer **D** — Section 1 of the Anti-social Behaviour Act 2003 deals with premises where drugs are used unlawfully:

(1) This section applies to premises if a police officer not below the rank of superintendent (the authorising officer) has reasonable grounds for believing —

(a) that at any time during the relevant period the premises have been used in connection with the unlawful use, production or supply of a Class A controlled drug, and

(b) that the use of the premises is associated with the occurrence of disorder or serious nuisance to members of the public.

So it's a Superintendent who authorises, not an assistant chief constable (ACC); answers A and C are incorrect. The relevant period over which the officer can consider the use of the club is also defined in the Act by s. 1(10): 'The relevant period is the period of three months ending with the day on which the authorising officer considers whether to authorise the issue of a closure notice in respect of the premises'. So three months, and not one month, is the appropriate period; answer B is therefore incorrect.

Crime, para. 1.6.7.11

Answer 5.16

Answer **B** — The secret is in the wording of the warrant: if the warrant only allows for searching of premises, that in itself will not give authority to search people on the premises unless the officer can point to some other authority allowing that search (see *Chief Constable of Thames Valley Police* v *Hepburn*, *The Times*, 19 December 2002). However, does that searching extend to everybody on the premises, even those there for an ancillary purpose? The Divisional Court has held that it is reasonable to restrict the movement of people within the premises to allow the search to be conducted properly (see *DPP* v *Meaden*, *The Times*, 2 January 2004). So the police can search the meter reader without his permission and can restrict his movements; answers A, C and D are therefore incorrect. After all, the officers only have his word that he is there to read meters (or am I cynical!)

Crime, para. 1.6.8.1

Answer 5.17

Answer **C** — Section 1 of the Anti-social Behaviour Act 2003 relates to closure notices. The police have power to close down premises being used for the supply, use or production of Class A drugs where there is associated serious nuisance or disorder. Section 4 of the Anti-social Behaviour Act 2003, which deals with offences relating to those closure notices, states:

> (1) A person commits an offence if he remains on or enters premises in contravention of a closure notice.
> (2) A person commits an offence if —
>> (a) he obstructs a constable or an authorised person acting under section 1(6) or 3(2),
>> (b) he remains on premises in respect of which a closure order has been made, or
>> (c) he enters the premises.

There is a statutory defence courtesy of s. 4(4):

> (4) But a person does not commit an offence under subsection (1) or subsection (2)(b) or (c) if he has a reasonable excuse for entering or being on the premises (as the case may be).

Therefore the offence is only complete where the person enters or remains on the premises with no reasonable excuse; answers A and D are therefore incorrect. This reasonable excuse defence does not exist where a constable or authorised person is obstructed; answer B is therefore incorrect as the offence is made out irrespective of any reasonable excuse proffered by the accused.

Crime, para. 1.6.7.15

Answer 5.18

Answer **B** — Section 28(2) allows a defence where the defendant did not know, suspect or have reason to suspect the existence of some fact which is essential to proving the case. In relation to this defence MILLIGAN could discharge the evidential burden by showing that he neither knew, nor suspected that the package contained a controlled drug, and that he neither knew nor suspected that he was supplying it to another. Both of these elements would be facts, which the prosecution would have to allege in order to prove the offence.

However external factors can impact on this defence. For example if MILLIGAN knew the person to be a local drug dealer, or the reward for his errand was suspiciously big, say £200!, then he may not be able to discharge this, albeit evidential, burden.

However it has been held that the test for 'reason to suspect' is an objective (factual) one (*R v Young* [1984] 1 WLR 654). Consequently, where a 'reason to suspect' was not apparent to a defendant because he/she was too intoxicated to see it, the defence will not apply. So if you're offered a package to deliver whilst drunk. . .

Consequently answers A, C and D are incorrect.

Crime, para. 1.6.6.3

Answer 5.19

Answer **B** — Possession of controlled drugs can be a complicated issue that is best summarised in the following way.

To prove possession of a controlled drug then you must show that a defendant both:

- had a controlled drug in his/her possession; and
- knew that he/she had something in his/her possession which was in fact a controlled drug.

So the accused had to have the controlled drug actually on them, they have to know they have it and finally they have to know it is a controlled drug. Without this the statutory defences come into play, which complicate matters even further, and a person would not be in possession of a controlled drug where:

- they had no knowledge that what they had in their possession was a controlled drug; answer A is therefore incorrect;
- they knew they had an item, and it transpired that item was in fact a controlled drug; answer C is therefore incorrect;
- they knew they had an item, and suspected that item was in fact a controlled drug; answer D is therefore incorrect.

In this scenario the person having the drugs in their pocket certainly had physical possession of them but without the requisite knowledge would not be in possession of a controlled drug.

Crime, paras 1.6.5.1, 1.6.5.2, 1.6.5.3

6 | Offences Against the Person

STUDY PREPARATION

This chapter deals with all non-fatal offences against the person, combining the relevant chapters of the *Blackstone's Police Manual*. This chapter examines the definition of assault and battery; it also addresses the offences of common assault, actual and grievous bodily harm, and the differences between them. Of particular importance in this area is the required element of state of mind (*mens rea*) and how that differs between offences.

Specific assaults in relation to police officers are considered, along with the less common offences of torture and poisoning. This chapter also covers the very serious offences of false imprisonment, kidnapping and hostage-taking. Although infrequently charged, these offences are perhaps of greater significance in the light of recent terrorist activity. This chapter should be read in conjunction with CPS Charging Standards.

QUESTIONS

Question 6.1

HAWKES is angry when the police attend at her house to arrest her son, and she follows the police out to their police car as they escort her son. Before they can stop her HAWKES jumps into the back seat of the police car next to her son and locks the door, refusing to leave; she is also very abusive to the officers verbally. Eventually she gets out of the police car and starts to walk off, still shouting obscenities at the officers. One of the officers approaches her and takes hold of her arm; she bites the officer and runs into her house, shutting the door behind her. The officers enter the premises by force and arrest HAWKES for an offence of assaulting a police officer contrary to the Police Act 1996, s. 89.

In relation to this which of the following is correct?

A The officers had lawful power to take hold of HAWKES's arm as she was committing a breach of the peace.

B The officers had lawful grounds to arrest HAWKES for assaulting a police officer, but had no power of entry to her house to effect it.

C The officers had lawful grounds to arrest HAWKES for assaulting a police officer, and there is a lawful power of entry to her house to effect it.

D The officers had no lawful grounds to arrest HAWKES and no power to enter even had the arrest been lawful.

Question 6.2

SMITH has been lawfully arrested for assault, where no actual force was used. In considering the legal definition of assault, what must be proved in order to convict SMITH of the offence?

A There must be intention to cause fear, although actual fear need not be proven.

B There can be recklessness as to fear caused and actual fear need not be proven.

C There must be fear of force being used, even though it may not be immediate.

D There must be fear of force being used and it must be immediate.

Question 6.3

DOUGHERTY takes her children to their dentist, WALKER. She consents to the children receiving fillings. During the procedure DOUGHERTY becomes concerned that WALKER is either drunk or drugged and reports the matter to the police. During the investigation is transpires that WALKER is taking drugs prescribed for a psychiatric illness, and for that reason he was suspended by the General Dental Council two months ago. The police are considering charging WALKER with assault.

Has WALKER unlawfully assaulted the children?

A No, DOUGHERTY has given true consent.

B No, any formal medical practice is not an assault.

C Yes, DOUGHERTY has given consent obtained by fraud.

D Yes, WALKER is suspended and no longer covered by law as it relates to consent.

Question 6.4

CHRITON stopped his car at a bus stop and told a lone women waiting for the bus that the bus had broken down about half a mile down the road (this was not in fact true). He offered the woman a lift. She accepted, but then asked to be let out of the car after a short distance. CHRITON refused and kept the woman in his car. He gets to his house and forces her down into the basement.

At what point, if any, does CHRITON 'kidnap' the woman?

A He does not kidnap her, she consents to get in the car.

B He kidnaps her when she first gets into the car.

C He kidnaps her when he refuses to let her out.

D He kidnaps her when he takes her into his house.

Question 6.5

SWALES is a store detective employed by a major retail chain. He witnesses a theft of a £200 cashmere sweater and follows the suspect, GRAINGER, outside the shop. SWALES holds GRAINGER and asks him to return to the shop as he has items for which he has not paid. GRAINGER pulls a knife and threatens SWALES with it. SWALES backs off and GRAINGER makes good his escape.

Has GRAINGER committed an offence of assault with intent to resist arrest under s. 38 of the Offences Against the Person Act 1861?

A No, as it applies to police officers making arrests only.

B No, as it applies to assaults involving actual injury only.

C Yes, as it applies to lawful arrests made by a person other than a constable.

D Yes, but only because s. 38 is triable only at Crown Court.

Question 6.6

Constable DOUGHTY wishes to question MILLS about an alleged assault. The officer attends at MILLS's home address and tells him the nature of the incident. Believing that he is about to be arrested, MILLS grabs hold of Constable DOUGHTY's arm and pulls him into the doorway; he then slams the door on the officer's arm and makes good his escape. As a result of this attack, Constable DOUGHTY's arm is broken in two places. When, interviewed, MILLS states that he did not intend to cause the injury, but accepts that his conduct presented a risk of some harm to the officer.

Which of the following statements is correct?

A This would not amount to a s. 18 assault, as there was no malice, i.e. premeditation.

B This would not amount to a s. 18 assault, as there was no intention to cause serious harm.

C This would amount to a s. 18 assault, as MILLS intended to prevent his lawful arrest.

D This would not amount to a s. 18 assault, as MILLS had not actually been arrested.

Question 6.7

PEARSON suspects that his wife is having an affair, as she goes out every Friday and Saturday night. She denies the allegation and intends to go out with her friends this Friday. When Friday comes, PEARSON follows her into town, goes into the club she is in, grabs hold of her and takes her back to his car about 100 metres down the road. His wife breaks free and runs back to her friends.

Has PEARSON committed the offence of kidnapping?

A No, as he only took her a short way.

B No, you cannot kidnap your spouse.

C No, he commits the offence of false imprisonment.

D Yes, all the elements of the offence are met.

Question 6.8

REES has had enough of her neighbour PATEY playing loud music at all hours of the day and night. One morning she took PATEY's milk from his doorstep. REES crushed eight sleeping tablets prescribed for her own use and put them in the milk, returning the bottle to PATEY's doorstep. REES knew exactly what she was doing and intended to make PATEY ill. The effects of the tablets were reduced by the milk, however, and they simply made PATEY fall asleep.

Has REES committed the offence of poisoning with intent under s. 24 of the Offences Against the Person Act 1861?

A Yes, as REES intended to injure, aggrieve or annoy PATEY.

B No, as the drugs are not 'noxious things'.

C Yes, provided that REES was at least reckless to any injury caused.

D No, as PATEY's life was never in danger.

Question 6.9

VICKERY is the Mayor of a small town and a strong advocate of European monetary union. Whilst leaving the town hall he sees STROUD writing graffiti all over the town hall, in more than 20 places prior to being seen by VICKERY. It stated, 'you can stick your Euros up your arse Vickery'. Incensed at this criminal damage (which would be more than £5,000), VICKERY makes an arrest and takes his prisoner back up into his office. In there he makes STROUD squat in the corner of his office and leaves him there for an hour. VICKERY then asks all 15 members of staff to come into the room at look at STROUD. They all laugh at him causing him extreme humiliation. VICKERY calls the police and STROUD is arrested by the police for criminal damage.

Which of the following statements is true?

A   VICKERY has not committed torture, as there was no real physical suffering by STROUD.

B   VICKERY has not committed torture, as he is not acting in the performance of his public duties.

C   VICKERY has committed torture, as he is a public official and has subjected STROUD to degrading treatment.

D   VICKERY and his staff members have all committed torture.

Question 6.10

TURNER has fallen out with his girlfriend following a heated argument. He sees her in town one afternoon with another man. TURNER's girlfriend is carrying her two-year-old son. TURNER punches his girlfriend on the nose, breaking it and making it bleed. At the time she is punched she drops the child, causing cuts and bruises to his face. TURNER then threatens his girlfriend's friend, who, fearing for his immediate safety, runs off.

In relation to this action, on whom has TURNER committed battery?

A   His girlfriend and her friend.

B   Only his girlfriend.

C   Both his girlfriend and the child.

D   All three of them.

Question 6.11

STEVENS is having an argument with BRIDGES in the street, opposite the police station. BRIDGES picks up a large piece of wood and raises it above his head. He says to STEVENS, 'How dare you swear at me. If we weren't opposite the nick I'd let you have this.'

Which of the following statements is correct?

A BRIDGES has committed an assault as he threatened to use immediate force.

B BRIDGES has committed an assault as he picked up a weapon.

C BRIDGES has not committed an assault as force was not actually used.

D BRIDGES has not committed an assault as his threat was negated by his words.

Question 6.12

FAULKNER is a Police Community Support Officer (PCSO) employed by her local Police Authority. Whilst on patrol she meets DALTON, who takes exception to her presence and wrestles her to the ground. CONNIKIE, a member of the public and very community-minded, tries to pull DALTON off of FAULKNER and DALTON responds by pushing CONNIKIE over.

Which of the following is true in relation to the Police Reform Act 2002?

A DALTON has committed an offence of assaulting a designated or accredited person in relation to both FAULKNER and CONNIKIE and can be arrested where that is deemed necessary by a police officer.

B DALTON has committed an offence of assaulting a designated or accredited person in relation to FAULKNER only and can be arrested where that is deemed necessary by a police officer.

C DALTON has committed an offence of assaulting a designated or accredited person in relation to both FAULKNER and CONNIKIE, and there is no power of arrest as it is not an indictable offence.

D DALTON has committed an offence of assaulting a designated or accredited person in relation to FAULKNER only, and there is no power of arrest as it is not an indictable offence.

Question 6.13

Constable RICHLEY is a black officer. She is making an arrest for a public order offence when the suspect pushes her to the ground, saying 'fuck you black bitch, get back to the jungle where you belong'. Constable RICHLEY is hurt but her injuries do not amount to a s. 47 assault.

The behaviour demonstrated by the offender amounts to racial or religious hatred. In relation to that, which of the following is true?

A In these circumstances the offender can *only* be charged with assault on police or assault with intent to resist arrest.

B The offender cannot be charged with a racially aggravated assault as this only applies to at least a s. 47 offence.

C The offender can be charged with racially aggravated common assault as the offence is made out.

D The offender can be charged with racially aggravated assault on police as the offence is made out.

Question 6.14

FARQUASON is infected with the HIV virus, and has unprotected sex with a woman he met in a nightclub. The woman consents fully to have sex with FARQUASON, and it was her idea not to use a condom. She contracts HIV as a direct result of this sexual encounter with FARQUASON.

Has FARQUASON committed an offence under s. 20 of the Offences Against the Person Act 1861?

A Yes, in these circumstances the offence is made out.

B Yes, provided the prosecution can show that FARQUASON had the relevant intent.

C No, as the woman should have been aware of the risk of having unprotected sex.

D No, as the woman consented to have sex and to have it unprotected.

Question 6.15

BARNES is facing a criminal prosecution for assault at the Crown Court. The incident occurred while BARNES was playing a football game, during which he tackled another player late, after the ball had been kicked out of play. The other player sustained a broken leg as a result of the tackle. BARNES has pleaded not guilty to the offence; his defence being that by playing football, the injured person had 'consented' to harm being done to him.

In relation to recent case law, which of the below are issues that the Court are *not* likely to take into consideration, when ruling on BARNES' defence?

A The level at which the game was being played.

B The state of mind of the accused at the time of the incident.

C Whether there had been any previous incidents between BARNES and the injured person during the game.

D The type of sport being played and the extent of risk of injury to the participants.

Question 6.16

The Children Act 2004 sets out to protect children from 'unreasonable punishment' by parents and carers.

Which of the following statements is correct, in relation to chastisement that *cannot* be justified as reasonable punishment under the above Act?

A The battery of a child under 17 cannot be justified if the injuries amount to an offence under ss. 18 or 20 of the Offences Against the Person Act 1861.

B The battery of a child under 18 cannot be justified if the injuries amount to an offence under ss. 18 or 20, or under s. 47 of the Offences Against the Person Act 1861.

C The battery of a child under 18 cannot be justified if the injuries amount to an offence under ss. 18 or 20 of the Offences Against the Person Act 1861.

D The battery of a child under 17 cannot be justified if the injuries amount to an offence under ss. 18 or 20, or under s. 47 of the Offences Against the Person Act 1861.

Question 6.17

CARPENTER has been knocked over by a car and has sustained injuries as a result of this deliberate act.

In relation to a possible 'assault' charge contrary to Offences Against the Person Act 1861 which of the following is correct?

A Although there are injuries, only relevant driving offences can be considered.

B An assault charge could be preferred as long as the injuries amounted to actual bodily harm (s. 47).

C An assault charge could be preferred as long as the injuries amounted to grievous bodily harm (s. 20).

D An assault charge could be preferred as long as the injuries amounted to grievous bodily harm with intent to do him grievous bodily harm (s. 18).

Question 6.18

COURTNEY and his girlfriend were having a stormy time in their relationship. COURTNEY was very upset when he discovered that she had been having an affair with her beauty therapist, who had helped manicure and keep her very long and polished nails. It had taken over two years to get her nails to the point where she thought they were perfect. Whilst she slept COURTNEY took some nail clippers and cut off one nail from each of his girlfriend's hands; needless to say she was less than happy and complained to the police that she had been assaulted.

In the circumstances as outlined above, would the actions of COURTNEY amount to an assault?

A This could only ever amount to a common assault, as she was asleep when the nails were cut.

B This could have amounted to assault occasioning actual bodily harm, but only if the girl had been awake and resisted the cutting.

C This could amount to assault occasioning actual bodily harm in these circumstances.

D This is not an assault at all; the nail beyond the cuticle is dead tissue, and in any event can be grown again.

Question 6.19

Constable PIPER was called to a road traffic collision, where a vehicle had driven into a wall and two men were seen running away from the scene. Constable PIPER made a search and saw HINCHCLIFFE nearby. The officer questioned HINCHCLIFFE about his movements, but he refused to answer any questions at all; however the officer could smell intoxicants. The officer discovered that HINCHCLIFFE was the registered owner of the vehicle from documents in his wallet and the officer asked under s. 172 of the Road Traffic Act 1988 for the name and address of the driver at the time of the collision, again with no verbal response from HINCHCLIFFE. He was eventually arrested for providing a positive sample of breath. Prior to being charged the police obtained irrefutable evidence that it was the other man who was driving, and not HINCHCLIFFE. In actual fact HINCHCLIFFE had sold the vehicle to the man who had been driving but he omitted to tell the police that.

Consider the offence of obstructing a police officer contrary to the Police Act 1996, s. 89; in these circumstances has HINCHCLIFFE committed this offence?

A Yes, for refusing to answer the direct questions asked only, but not for omitting to volunteer information.

B Yes, for refusing to answer the direct questions asked only, and also for omitting to volunteer information.

C No, the offence of obstruction cannot be committed by simply failing to answer questions or by omitting to volunteer information.

D No, as there must be at least some form of physical resistance, even where refusing to answer questions or by omitting to volunteer information.

ANSWERS

Answer 6.1

Answer **D** — It is critical to the offence of assaulting a police officer contrary to the Police Act 1996, s. 89 that the officer was acting in the execution of his/her duty when assaulted. Given the almost infinite variety of situations that police officers may find themselves in, it is difficult to define the precise boundaries of the execution of their duty; however through decided cases the courts have assisted to define what is, and more importantly, what is not lawful execution.

In *R (on the Application of Hawkes)* v *DPP* [2005] EWHC 3046, the defendant was convicted of assaulting a police officer in the execution of his duty after the police had gone to her home address to arrest her son. After the arrest, the defendant followed her son into a police car and refused to get out. She was given a warning and was verbally abusive, and only got out of the car when a second police car arrived. The defendant then started to walk towards her house but a police officer took hold of her arms. She bit the police officer on the arm. The prosecution case was that the police officer had arrested her for a breach of the peace and that the assault had occurred in the execution of that duty. The defendant argued that the prosecution case had been that she had actually committed a breach of the peace whilst she had been sitting in the police car. It was not a case of a threatened breach; accordingly, there was a requirement to establish some sort of violent conduct. Allowing her appeal, the Divisional Court held that the defendant had exhibited nothing more than an aggressive manner and that, while her conduct may have given rise to an imminent threat of violence, there was no evidence to suggest that it involved any violence justifying the conclusion that she had actually committed a breach of the peace in the presence of the police officer. In the circumstances, her arrest had been unlawful and the conviction for assaulting a police officer in the execution of his duty could not stand.

This question of the lawfulness of any arrest will become even more important to this offence (s. 89) in light of the re-wording of s. 24 of the Police and Criminal Evidence Act 1984 following the Serious Organised Crime and Police Act 2005. An offence contrary to s. 89 is a summary only offence, therefore the general power of entry under s. 17(1) of the Police and Criminal Evidence Act 1984 will not apply.

There is no power of arrest as no offence has been committed, and in any case there is no power of entry to effect the arrest (even had it been lawful); answers A, B and C are therefore incorrect.

Crime, para. 1.8.3.3

Answer 6.2

Answer **D** — There has to be intentional or reckless causation of the fear of force, but the fear of force is the key to assault, which makes answers A and B incorrect. An assault requires conduct which causes the victim to apprehend the immediate use of unlawful force upon him. The concept of immediacy has nevertheless been interpreted with some flexibility, and there have been a number of recent cases in which 'stalkers' have been prosecuted for assault on that basis. In *Smith* v *Chief Superintendent, Woking Police Station* (1983) 76 Cr App R 234, the Divisional Court held that a threat of violence could be considered immediate, even though the accused was still outside the victim's home, looking in at her through a window, and would have needed to force an entry before he could attack her. This, however, relates to the time period and not the victim's actual fear, which remains as the fear of immediate use of unlawful force, and therefore answer C is incorrect.

Crime, paras 1.8.2.4, 1.8.2.5

Answer 6.3

Answer **A** — This question deals with consent and broadly follows the outline of the circumstances in the case of *R* v *Richardson* [1999] QB 444. In that case it was held that a dentist's failure to inform patients that the General Dental Council had suspended him did not affect the true 'consent' given for medical treatment (answer D is incorrect). In *Richardson*, Otton LJ held that there had been no deception as to the identity of the dentist, or the nature of the act carried out, and this therefore could not vitiate consent and there could be no assault. Consent obtained by fraud would relate to the identity of the dentist as a trained dentist, which is not the case here, and answer C is therefore incorrect. Consent to medical treatment is true consent, but going beyond agreed treatment could be an assault, e.g. the indecent touching of the patient, and thus answer B is incorrect.

Crime, para. 1.8.2.6

Answer 6.4

Answer **B** — Kidnapping is defined at common law as 'the taking or carrying away of one person by another without the consent of the person so taken or carried away, and without lawful excuse'.

The issue here is consent, and certainly the woman consents to get into the car. However, the Court of Appeal held in *R* v *Cort* [2003] 3 WLR 1300, that if the consent is obtained by fraud, as it was here through the lies told, then this would not be true consent. Without such consent, the offence is made out when the woman gets in the car and, as CHRITON has kidnapped her, answer A is incorrect. Although he further detains her, this is more the offence of false imprisonment, and happens after she is kidnapped; answers C and D are therefore incorrect.

Crime, para. 1.9.5

Answer 6.5

Answer **C** — On a literal reading of s. 38 of the Offences Against the Person Act 1861, the only *actus reus* required is that of common assault, making answer B incorrect, whereas the *mens rea* is that of common assault, coupled with an intent to resist or prevent one's own, or another person's, lawful arrest or detention. Nevertheless, it is firmly established that the arrest or detention in question must in fact be lawful (*R* v *Self* [1992] 3 All ER 476; *R* v *Lee* [2000] Crim LR 991) and this is an essential element. The person making the arrest (or trying to) need not be a police officer as s. 110 of the Serious Organised Crime and Police Act 2005 gives a power of arrest to a person other than a constable where an indictable offence has been committed. As s. 38 is an either way offence it fits within the Serious Organised Crime and Police Act 2005 definition of 'indictable offence', which makes answers A and D incorrect.

Crime, para. 1.8.3.2

Answer 6.6

Answer **C** — 'Maliciously' does not need premeditation but rather amounts to subjective recklessness, and the suspect admits this. He accepts that there was a risk of harm. He does not have to foresee the degree of harm and therefore answer A is incorrect. This offence has two strands:

- An intention to cause serious harm; *or*
- An intention to resist or prevent lawful apprehension.

Where, in contrast, it is alleged that the defendant merely intended to resist arrest etc., malice becomes an important further element to be proved, and therefore answer B is incorrect. It applies to intention to prevent as well as resist arrest, and not just when someone has actually been arrested, and therefore D is incorrect.

Crime, para. 1.8.4.3

Answer 6.7

Answer **D** — The offences of false imprisonment, kidnapping and hostage-taking are very closely linked, in fact the state of mind required is the same. In *R v Rahman* (1985) 81 Cr App R 349, it was stated that the *mens rea* for false imprisonment is intentional or reckless restraint of a person's movement (recklessness here means subjective recklessness). Answer C is incorrect, as PEARSON has not restrained his wife's movement. You can kidnap your spouse, as you could kidnap any person, provided the basic definition of the offence is met (*R v Reid* [1973] QB 299) and therefore answer B is incorrect. Also, the distance taken may only be a short one (*R v Wellard* [1978] 3 All ER 161) and therefore answer A is incorrect.

Crime, paras 1.9.5, 1.9.7

Answer 6.8

Answer **A** — The offence is one of specific intent, and recklessness is not sufficient, so answer C is incorrect. In *R v Marcus* [1981] 2 All ER 833, the Court of Appeal held that a substance which might be harmless in small quantities could therefore be 'noxious' if the quantity administered was sufficient to injure, aggrieve or annoy (answer B is incorrect). Section 24 is distinguished from s. 23 of the 1861 Act, in that the latter requires proof of a consequence — namely, the endangering of a person's life or the infliction of grievous bodily harm — and therefore answer D is incorrect.

Crime, paras 1.9.3, 1.9.3.1

Answer 6.9

Answer **B** — VICKERY does not appear to be acting in the performance or purported performance of his duties, and therefore cannot be guilty of torture (answer C is incorrect). It might be argued that he saw his actions as being part of his civic managerial duties, but this is unlikely to succeed. The meaning of 'severe pain or suffering' does not have to amount to grievous bodily harm, actual bodily harm or any standard measured by degree of injury. Indeed, the wording of s. 134(3) of the Criminal Justice Act 1988 provides that the pain or suffering may be purely mental. It is the severity of the pain rather than whether or not identifiable injury results that should be considered, though evidence of injury would be admissible evidence of the severity of the pain. Answer A is therefore incorrect. The arguments against the actions of VICKERY falling within the scope of his public duties apply even more clearly to the actions of his staff, and therefore answer D is also incorrect.

Crime, para. 1.9.2

Answer 6.10

Answer **C** — A battery requires the unlawful application of force upon the victim, so, although the male friend has been assaulted, he has not been 'battered'. Answers A and D are therefore wrong. Where someone strikes another causing her to drop and injure her child, it has been held to be a battery against both (*Haystead* v *Chief Constable of Derbyshire* [2000] 3 All ER 890). As the child has also been assaulted, answer B is incorrect.

Crime, para. 1.8.2.2

Answer 6.11

Answer **D** — Words used by the accused may indicate that no real attack is imminent, even where the circumstances might suggest otherwise. This principle has been clearly established since the very ancient case of *Tuberville* v *Savage* (1669) 1 Mod 3, where, in the course of a quarrel with S, T placed his hand on the hilt of his sword (an act which might ordinarily have been construed as an assault) and exclaimed, 'If it were not assize time, I would not take such language from you'. 'Assize time' meant that the judges were in town, and no doubt T feared being arrested and tried. The same principle applies on the facts of this question where BRIDGES makes a 'qualified' threat to STEVENS (answers A and B are therefore incorrect). As a point of interest the older the case law the better law it is, as it has stood the test of time, over 330 years in this case! There can be assault where no force is used, i.e. threats making the other person fear immediate attack, and therefore answer C is incorrect.

Crime, para. 1.8.2.3

Answer 6.12

Answer **A** — The Police Reform Act 2002, s. 46(1) states:

(1) Any person who assaults —
    (a) a designated person in the execution of his duty,
    (b) an accredited person in the execution of his duty, or
    (c) a person assisting a designated or accredited person in the execution of his duty,
is guilty of an offence.

Provided the designated or accredited person was acting in the execution of his or her duty, it is an offence to assault either that person or anyone assisting him or her, therefore answers B and D are incorrect as they state that only the PCSO is assaulted.

By virtue of the Serious Organised Crime and Police Act 2005 all offences are arrestable where deemed necessary by a police officer because certain criteria are met. However powers of arrest are also extended to 'any person' but only where an indictable offence is involved, s. 46(1) of the Police Reform Act is summary only; answer C is therefore incorrect.

Crime, para. 1.8.3.5

Answer 6.13

Answer **C** — Although the offences of assault on police (s. 89 of the Police Act 1996) and assault with intent to resist arrest (s. 38 of the Offences Against the Person Act 1861) are perfectly valid for this instance, given the racially aggravated factors a more serious charge is appropriate. Also answer A also says can *only* be charged, precluding any other offence such as common assault, which is not true, and for that reason answer A is incorrect. In *R* v *Jacobs* [2001] 2 Cr App R (S) 174, a female police officer was subjected to repeated verbal racial abuse by a female suspect who had been arrested and taken to the police station. Bennett J commented that 'police officers are entitled to be protected, just as any other members of the public, from racial abuse'. And the Crime and Disorder Act 1998 extends this racially aggravating factor to various levels of assault, common assault being one of them (s. 29(1)(c) of the 1998 Act), therefore answer B is incorrect. It does not extend such offences to the Police Act, however, and there is no such offence of racially aggravated assault on police; answer D is therefore incorrect.

Crime, para. 1.8.3.1

Answer 6.14

Answer **A** — Section 20 of the Offences Against the Person Act 1861 does not require intent to commit grievous bodily harm (GBH), that is a s. 18 offence, and the prosecution only have to show that the accused unlawfully and maliciously inflicted GBH, therefore answer B is incorrect. Certainly contracting HIV could be said to be an 'injury resulting in some permanent disability' and as such amounts to GBH; the issue here is consent. In *R* v *Dica* [2004] EWCA Crim 1103, it was held that recklessness to consent, as such, was not in issue. In *Dica* the defendant had unprotected sex with two women, knowing he was HIV positive. Although both women were willing to have sexual intercourse with the defendant, the prosecution's case was that their agreement would never have been given if they had known of the defendant's condition. The defendant stated that he told both women of his condition, and that they were nonetheless willing to have sexual intercourse with him. However, the judge ruled that whether or not the complainants knew of the defendant's condition, their consent, if any, was irrelevant and provided no defence, since *R v Brown* [1994] 1 AC 212 deprived the complainants of the legal capacity to consent to such serious harm. In *Brown* it was held that sado-masochistic acts which occurred in private and which were consented to could found charges under the 1861 Act, ss. 20 and 47, if the injuries, though not permanent, were neither transient nor trifling. So, irrespective of the victim's willingness to place herself at risk, or to consent to sexual activity, FARQUASON has committed the offence; answers C and D are therefore incorrect.

Crime, paras 1.8.2.6, 1.8.4.2

Answer 6.15

Answer **C** — The Court of Appeal examined the issue of 'consent to injury' in the case of *R v Barnes* [2004] EWCA Crim 3246. The case was similar to the circumstances in this question and, while accepting that the tackle was hard, the defendant claimed that it had been a fair challenge and that the injury was caused accidentally. The Court held that, if the actions of the defendant had been within the rules of the game being played, it would be a firm indication that what had occurred was not criminal.

However, in relation to the *Barnes* case, the Court held that the threshold level was an objective one to be determined by:

- the type of sport being played;
- the level at which it was being played;
- the nature of the 'act';
- the degree of force used;
- the extent of risk of injury to the participants; and
- the state of mind of the defendant.

The issue of whether there had been any previous incidents between the accused and the injured person during the game was not considered during this ruling; therefore since all the other issues listed are matters that the Court *did* consider, answers A, B and D are incorrect.

Crime, paras 1.8.3.3, 1.8.4.2, 1.8.4.3

Answer 6.16

Answer **B** — Section 58 of the Children Act 2004 provides that the battery of a person under 18 years of age (not 17, therefore answers A and D are incorrect) cannot be justified on the ground that it constituted reasonable punishment in relation to an offence under ss. 47, 18 or 20 of the Offences Against the Person Act 1861. Since all three of the above offences are covered, answers A and C are incorrect.

Crime, para. 1.8.2.7

Answer 6.17

Answer **B** — The Court of Appeal has held, in the case of *R* v *Bain* [2005] EWCA Crim 07, that there is nothing wrong on principle in charging a driver with causing grievous bodily harm as well as dangerous driving in appropriate circumstances; answer A is therefore incorrect. It follows that bringing about other forms of lasting or significant injury with a motor vehicle could also be so charged, leaving the starting point at actual bodily harm (s. 47); consequently answers C and D are incorrect.

Crime, para. 1.8.4

Answer 6.18

Answer **C** — It must be shown that 'actual bodily harm' was a consequence, directly or indirectly, of the defendant's actions. Such harm can include shock (*R* v *Miller* [1954] 2 QB 282) and mental 'injury' (*R* v *Chan-Fook* [1994] 1 WLR 689).

So what is 'actual bodily harm'? In *DPP* v *Smith* [1961] AC 290, it was noted that the expression needed 'no explanation' and, in *Chan-Fook*, the court advised that the phrase consisted of 'three words of the English language which require no elaboration and in the ordinary course should not receive any'. So actual bodily harm appears to mean what it says. But that is not necessarily as clear as it sounds.

In *DPP* v *Smith (Ross Michael)* [2006] EWHC 94 the Divisional Court took the view that in light of there being no prior decisions directly in point that cutting off a person's hair can amount to actual bodily harm; answer D is therefore incorrect.

The Court viewed that:

> It is necessary to look at definitions because there is nothing to assist us in the decided cases. In ordinary language, 'harm' is not limited to 'injury', and according to the Concise Oxford Dictionary extends to 'hurt' or 'damage'. According to the same dictionary, 'bodily', whether used as an adjective or an adverb, is 'concerned with the body'. 'Actual', as defined in the authorities, means that the bodily harm should not be so trivial or trifling as to be effectively without significance.

Sir Igor Judge (President of the Queen's Bench Division) stated in *Smith (Ross Michael)*:

> In my judgment, whether it is alive beneath the surface of the skin or dead tissue above the surface of the skin, the hair is an attribute and part of the human body. It is intrinsic to each individual and to the identity of each individual. Although it is not essential to my decision, I note that an individual's hair is relevant to his or her autonomy. Some regard it as their crowning glory. Admirers may so regard it in the object of their affections. Even if, medically and scientifically speaking, the hair above the surface of the scalp is no more than dead tissue, it remains part of the body and is attached to it. While it is so attached, in my judgment it falls within the meaning of 'bodily' in the phrase 'actual bodily harm'. It is concerned with the body of the individual victim.

This case is identical to this scenario as nails and hair would be said to be synonymous. So although also being a common assault, there would be a case to answer for a s. 47 assault, and this is the case whether the person was asleep or awake; answers A and B are therefore incorrect.

Crime, para. 1.8.4.1

Answer 6.19

Answer **B** — Under s. 89(2) of the Police Act 1996, any person who resists or wilfully obstructs a constable in the execution of his/her duty, or a person assisting a constable in the execution of his/her duty, shall be guilty of an offence.

Resistance suggests some form of physical opposition; obstruction does not and may take many forms; answer D is therefore incorrect. Obstruction has been interpreted as making it more difficult for a constable to carry out his/her duty (*Hinchcliffe v Sheldon* [1955] 1 WLR 1207) and refusing to answer an officer's questions is not obstruction (*Rice v Connolly* [1966] 2 QB 414) — *unless the defendant was under some duty to provide information*. In this scenario the defendant was under not only a duty, but a legal requirement, to provide information; answer C is therefore incorrect.

Similarly, obstruction can be caused by omission but only where the defendant was already under some duty towards the police or the officer, and by omitting to provide information that he had that he was under a duty to disclose would be evidence of 'obstruction' by omission; answer A is therefore incorrect.

Crime, para. 1.8.3.4

7 | Sexual Offences

STUDY PREPARATION

Sexual offences cover a wide range of activities. In answering these questions there is a real need first of all to identify who is doing what to whom. Usually the key to the offences that arise from such activities is to be found in:

- the ages of the parties;
- the intent of the offender;
- the consent of the victim;
- the accompanying circumstances.

Until fairly recently sexual offences were subject to an Act almost half a century old — ask yourself, have sexual activity and attitudes changed since then? The existing framework was described as 'archaic, incoherent and discriminatory'. The resulting Sexual Offences Act 2003 is a landmark statute that repealed almost all of the Sexual Offences Act 1956 and many other statutory provisions enacted since, delivering, in effect, a new criminal code of sexual offences. The Sexual Offences Act 2003 not only introduces a considerable number of new offences and criminalises certain types of conduct not previously subjected to the written law, it also substantially redefines many sex crimes, incorporating new terms and language deemed more appropriate to contemporary society.

QUESTIONS

Question 7.1

FERGUSON met a girl at a party and she agreed to go back to his house. At FERGUSON'S house the girl agrees to have sexual intercourse with him, and they both consume a lot of alcohol; the girl is very drunk. FERGUSON goes to the bathroom, and prior to his return the girl falls asleep on the bed. FERGUSON has sex with her while she sleeps.

Has FERGUSON committed rape?

A No as she agreed to sex prior to falling asleep.

B No, as her drunkenness was self-induced.

C Yes, even although she earlier agreed.

D Yes, but only if the prosecution prove lack of real consent.

Question 7.2

JENKINSON is sexually attracted to his male colleague, COLLINS. One night JENKINSON persuades COLLINS to go back to his house, where he thinks he will be able to have sex with him; and to ensure sex takes place, JENKINSON plies COLLINS with alcohol and adds drugs to the drink to stupefy COLLINS. COLLINS becomes all but unconscious; JENKINSON then inserts his penis into COLLINS' mouth.

What offence, if any, has JENKINSON committed?

A Rape.

B Assault by penetration.

C Administering a substance with intent?

D Causing a person to engage in sexual activity without consent.

Question 7.3

DAWSON, a woman, is lying in the local park one summer's day. Feeling aroused, she begins to masturbate herself, openly, and the park is very busy. Several people walk by and see DAWSON; her vagina is clearly visible, but no one is offended by this behaviour. DAWSON was only intending self-pleasure.

Has DAWSON committed the offence of exposure?

A Yes, as she exposed her genitals in public.

B Yes, as she exposed her genitals in public and people can see her.

C No, as no one was offended by the behaviour.

D No, as she did not intend anyone to be caused alarm or distress.

Question 7.4

BRIAN is 15 years of age, but is a mature boy who looks older than he is. He has been infatuated with his neighbour's 25-year-old daughter for some time, and wishes to have sex with her. One night they are alone in BRIAN's house and he starts to seduce her; she freely consents. They do not have sexual intercourse, but she masturbates BRIAN.

Which of the following is correct?
A The woman has committed a sexual assault.
B The woman has committed an offence of sexual activity with a child.
C The woman has committed no offence, as the boy consented to the act.
D The woman has committed no offence, as no intercourse took place.

Question 7.5

STRUTHERS and his girlfriend, who are both 17 years of age, are in their bedroom and are joined by STRUTHERS' younger brother, who is 13 years of age. Whilst the brother watches, STRUTHERS and his girlfriend participate in mutual masturbation and oral sex. They both know the child is present, and both are getting sexual gratification from the fact they are being watched by the brother. The brother is not offended and enjoys watching.

Is this engaging in sexual activity in the presence of a child contrary to s. 11 of the Sexual Offences Act 2003?
A Yes, as they are over 17 years of age.
B Yes, because the brother is under 14 years of age.
C No, because they are not 18 years of age or over.
D No, because the child is not offended, nor forced to watch.

Question 7.6

GUNN invites DAVIES, who is 19 and suffering from a severe mental disorder, back to his house. GUNN then asks DAVIES to take all his clothes off, which he willingly does. Because of his mental disorder DAVIES is unable to refuse involvement in sexual activity. GUNN then tries to penetrate DAVIES anally, which DAVIES has freely agreed to. GUNN only just manages to penetrate DAVIES, then gives up and sends DAVIES home.

In order to prove the offence of sexual activity with a person with a mental disorder (s. 30), what does the prosecution have to show?
A That GUNN knew DAVIES suffered from a mental disorder.
B That GUNN knew DAVIES suffered from a mental disorder and knew he was unlikely to refuse his advances.

C That GUNN used inducements to get DAVIES to agree to the touching.

D That GUNN coerced DAVIES into agreeing to the touching.

Question 7.7

DOOLEY's computer was found to contain thousands of indecent images of children. Most had been downloaded via an Internet file-sharing system whereby members installed software allowing files, held in their shared folder, to be accessed and downloaded directly into shared folders of other members whilst connected to the Internet. Only six of all the files downloaded were found in the defendant's shared folder, in respect of which he was charged with six counts of possessing indecent photographs or pseudo-photographs of a child with a view to their being distributed or shown by himself or others, contrary to s. 1(1)(c) of the Protection of Children Act 1978.

The defendant contended that he did not intend to distribute or show the photographs to others and, once downloaded, he usually moved the files into folders not accessible to other members. The six files in the shared folder had not yet been moved due to the process he used to download and move images in bulk.

Considering the offence contrary to s. 1(1)(c) of the Protection of Children Act 1978 has DOOLEY committed this offence?

A The images in the shared folder were possessed with a view to their being distributed, and he is guilty.

B The images are being held in a file that could be accessed by other members and DOOLEY is aware of this, and therefore he is guilty.

C The images are stored with a view to moving them to a private folder and as such he is not guilty of this offence.

D The images are not stored with an intention of allowing the distribution of them and as such he is not guilty of the offence.

Question 7.8

STEPHENSON, 22 years old, is a convicted child sex offender currently on parole. He is seen by concerned parents every day of the week standing outside a local primary school. He does or says nothing, but is always outside the school when the children are released.

What is the fullest extent to which a risk of sexual harm order (RSHO) may be made to protect children?

A To protect all the children at the school who are at risk from STEPHENSON.

B To protect a particular child at the school who is at risk from STEPHENSON.
C To protect any child in the locality who is at risk from STEPHENSON.
D To protect any child anywhere who is at risk from STEPHENSON.

Question 7.9

YOUNG lives with his prostitute girlfriend and has recently encouraged her to go to work as a prostitute for DIBLEY, a local drug dealer. YOUNG hopes that in providing his girlfriend, DIBLEY will supply him with cheap drugs in the future, which is likely. YOUNG receives no money from DIBLEY for the deal. His girlfriend is happy with this arrangement, as she will make more money working for DIBLEY.

Has YOUNG committed an offence of controlling prostitution for gain under s. 53 of the Sexual Offences Act 2003?

A No, there has been no gain as yet, only future hopes of gain.
B No, as YOUNG's girlfriend is not forced into prostitution.
C Yes, as there will be future financial advantage.
D Yes, as the prostitute will make money and she lives with YOUNG.

Question 7.10

MARKS and his female secretary, HIRST, attended a conference in Blackpool. While they were there, MARKS tried to get HIRST to have sex with him. She refused and MARKS got angry. He told her that if she didn't have sex with him, he would beat her husband up with a hammer when they got back home. Fearing for her husband's safety, HIRST had sex with MARKS. In fact MARKS had no intention of harming her husband.

Has MARKS committed rape?

A Yes, as MARKS threatened violence against HIRST's husband.
B Yes, as HIRST only consented through MARKS' deception.
C No, as the violence threatened was not immediate.
D No, as the violence threatened was not against HIRST.

Question 7.11

BROADHURST and his girlfriend LAWRENCE are having anal sex in a toilet cubicle in a mens toilet. Another man enters the toilet and hears what he clearly believes to be a couple having sex; he laughs and leaves the toilet.

Regarding sexual activity in a public lavatory, which of the following is true?

A This offence is not made out because no one was offended or disgusted.

B This offence is not made out as they are not engaged in homosexual sex.

C This offence is made out only because it involves anal sex.

D This offence is made out and both are guilty of it.

Question 7.12

PEARD was given a caution for being a common prostitute, and asks you if she can dispute the interpretation of her actions as being 'soliciting'.

Which of the following is correct?

A No, she cannot dispute the caution, as it is not an official caution for an offence.

B No, she cannot dispute the caution, as it is only recorded in a police held register.

C Yes, she can apply to a court within 7 days of the caution.

D Yes, she can apply to a court within 14 days of the caution.

Question 7.13

TURNER is a convicted paedophile, and notified police of his home address. He has stayed with a friend some 300 miles from his home address; he stayed with this friend for 3 days, 2 months ago, and now intends spending another 3 days with him. He has not notified police of the address of his friend.

Should he now notify police that he is staying with his friend?

A No, as he is not staying there for 7 days.

B No, as he has not stayed there for 7 days in the last year.

C Yes, he must notify police of any place he is staying, for any period.

D Yes, he is away from his notified address for more than 2 days.

Question 7.14

BAKER is a man who wishes to pay a prostitute for sexual intercourse. He has never done this before and is a bit unsure what to do. He gets into his car and drives to a residential area he believes, mistakenly, to be a well-known red light area. He notices a lone woman standing near the bus stop; he stops beside her and says 'Are you doing business?'. Not knowing what he means she says 'No I'm waiting for a bus, what sort of business are you looking for?' Confused, BAKER drives straight home.

Which of the following is correct?

A He has committed an offence of kerb-crawling as his behaviour is likely to cause annoyance to the woman.

B He has committed an offence of kerb-crawling as he has solicited the woman from his car.

C He has not committed an offence of kerb-crawling as the woman was not offended.

D He has not committed an offence of kerb-crawling as he did not intend to cause annoyance to the woman.

Question 7.15

CLINTON has a 15-year-old daughter, KAREN, who looks older than her age. CLINTON introduced KAREN to his friend, GEORGE, who is a pimp. Between them, CLINTON and GEORGE persuaded KAREN to become a prostitute. She agreed and went out with GEORGE on weekends only, and solicited in the street for prostitution. KAREN's mother was aware of what was happening to her daughter and encouraged her, but refused to accept any money from what the child earned.

In relation to offences under s. 48 of the Sexual Offences Act 2003 of causing or inciting child prostitution, which of the following is true?

A GEORGE has committed the offence, but CLINTON has not.

B CLINTON has committed the offence, but GEORGE has not.

C CLINTON and GEORGE have committed the offence in these circumstances.

D CLINTON, GEORGE and the child's mother have committed the offence.

Question 7.16

PORTER downloaded some pornographic pictures of children under the age of 16 from the Internet. He took them to work and lent them to his friend, WILLIS, who returned them the next day.

Who has committed an offence in relation to the photographs?

A Both: PORTER for possessing and distributing photographs; WILLIS for being in possession of them.

B Only PORTER, for possessing and distributing the photographs to another person.

C Both PORTER and WILLIS for possession, as photographs cannot be distributed to just one person in this way.

D Both PORTER and WILLIS for possession, as the offence of distributing does not include lending.

Question 7.17

PAVETT is a woman employed as a cleaner at an NHS hospital specialising in mental health. She is sexually very active and is caught one morning having sexual intercourse with a male patient, who was receiving treatment for a mental disorder at the hospital as an outpatient. The man is a regular outpatient, and PAVETT frequently sees him on a daily basis. Consider s. 39 of the Sexual Offences Act 2003, on care workers causing or inciting sexual activity.

In relation to PAVETT's actions, which of the following is correct?

A She has committed this offence as she is a care worker.

B She has committed the offence: even though she is not a care worker, the man is an outpatient.

C She has not committed the offence as she is not a care worker.

D She has not committed the offence because the man is an outpatient.

Question 7.18

COLLINS is very keen to have sexual intercourse with BETTY. She tells him she is only interested in his friendship and wants nothing more than that. One night COLLINS decides that she will have sex with him if he forces the issue, so he hides outside her bedroom window on the ledge, intent on entering and having sex with BETTY. He intends to force her to have sex, although he honestly believes she wants to. He breaks the window and enters the house. She is, however, not in the house.

Which of the following is true in relation to the Sexual Offences Act 2003, regarding COLLINS' intent?

A COLLINS commits an offence when he breaks the bedroom window.

B COLLINS commits an offence when he hides outside the bedroom window.

C COLLINS does not commit an offence, as he has an honest belief and no sex took place.

D COLLINS does not commit an offence, as Betty was not in the house.

Question 7.19

WISE, aged 48 years, owns a sweet shop, which he uses to further his paedophilic desires. He sees BEN, who is 12 years old, in the shop and has desires to touch him sexually. He arranges to meet BEN later in the local park. He has never met BEN before. He walks to the park at about 7 p.m., and meets BEN by the swings. BEN realises something is wrong and runs off before WISE can touch him.

At what point, if any, does WISE commit an offence under s. 15 of the Sexual Offences Act 2003, on child grooming?

A When he arranges to meet the child.

B When he starts walking to meet the child.

C When he first meets the child in the park.

D He does not commit the offence as he has not previously communicated with the child.

Question 7.20

GIBBONS is a biology teacher at the local High School, and SIAN is a 16-year-old pupil in his class. They are very friendly and SIAN adores GIBBONS, and they converse frequently in an Internet chatroom. GIBBONS sends indecent still photographs in an e-mail to SIAN's school computer terminal from his; they are very explicit pictures. SIAN loves the pictures and is not in the least concerned by them. GIBBONS receives sexual gratification from knowing that SIAN looks at the pictures, and if questioned by the school he will say it is part of a sex education programme.

Has GIBBONS committed an offence under s. 19 of the Sexual Offences Act 2003 on abuse of position of trust causing a child to watch a sexual act?

A Yes, but only because SIAN is a pupil in his class.

B Yes, but only because of the sexual gratification he gets.

C No, this offence only applies to a child under 16 years of age.

D No, because they are still pictures and not a 'moving image'.

Question 7.21

TURNER is the manager of a gym, and has recently been subject to a number of thefts of personal property from clients using the sun beds. To combat this he gets permission from all the clientele to install a hidden camera in this area. The clients agree to the camera recording the activities in this area of the gym, and for it to be viewed by the police should a further theft occur. No permission was obtained for DOOLEY to view the recording 'live'. All the clientele also agree to wear underwear during the time the camera is installed. A camera is installed and begins to record; unknown to the clientele DOOLEY has a fetish about women walking round in their underwear and although his original intention was to try to catch the thief he now starts to watch the recording 'live' expressly for his own sexual gratification.

In these circumstances had DOOLEY committed an offence of voyeurism contrary to the Sexual Offences Act 2003, s. 67?

A No, as he has permission from the clients to film them and as such cannot commit this offence.

B No, as the persons using the sun beds are wearing underwear and not exposing any part of their 'private' areas.

C Yes, although he had permission to film he did not have permission to view the video 'live'.

D Yes, as the clientele were unaware of the purpose formed after the camera was installed he commits this offence.

Question 7.22

TURNER has been convicted of possessing indecent photographs of a child, and has changed his home address since being released from prison, having served his sentence.

How should this notification of change of address be made?

A Must be personally at the police station.

B Can be by sending written notification.

C Can be by sending written notification or by telephoning the station.

D Must be by written notification.

Question 7.23

A Sexual Offences Prevention Order is made with a view to prohibiting a defendant from doing 'anything' described in that order.

To what sort of activity does this 'anything' apply?

A Any criminal activity relating to his previous convictions.

B Any criminal activity; the person does not have to have previous convictions.

C Any criminal activity or civil wrong; the person does not have to have previous convictions.

D Any criminal activity or civil wrong.

Question 7.24

A 17-year-old male has been made subject to a Notification Order by virtue of the Sexual Offences Act 2003 and the court has further ordered a parental direction. The young male has failed to comply with the order by not attending at the police station to report a change of address. His parents tried many times to get him to attend at the police station, even trying to physically take him there.

Has an offence been committed by the parent made subject of the parental direction in relation to an offence of failure to notify contrary to s. 91 of the Sexual Offences Act 2003?

A Yes, as they failed to comply with the parental direction irrespective of their actions.

B Yes, as they failed to comply with the parental direction as they should have attended at the police station themselves with the change of address.

C No, only the male subject to the order commits an offence of failure to notify; a parental order does not apply to this notification.

D No, as the offence is only committed by a person with no reasonable excuse and the parents are likely to have such excuse.

Question 7.25

GREATREX is a 32-year-old female. She was walking down the street when a male, ROBINS approached her and said 'any chance of a blow job darling?'. GREATREX walked away, but was approached again by ROBINS who asked if she was shy or a lesbian. ROBINS then tried to pull GREATREX towards him by grabbing at a pocket that was located at the side seam of GREATREX's trousers. GREATREX is greatly offended by this and she believes it to be sexual.

Is this an offence of sexual touching contrary to s. 3 of the Sexual Offences Act 2003?

A No, because ROBINS did not touch a part of the body itself as is required by the legislation.

B No, because ROBINS did not touch a sexual organ as is required by the legislation.

C Yes, because of the purpose of ROBINS' actions and 'touching' includes clothing.

D Yes, because GREATREX thought that it was sexual and 'touching' includes clothing.

Question 7.26

WILLIAMS receives an email from a friend that includes an attachment he knows contains pornographic images. He downloads and then opens the attachment, which is several pages long. He views adult females engaged in various sexual activities and then leaves the room where the computer is. On the page after the one he was looking at are several images of children that are indecent in content. WILLIAMS is unaware that there are sexually explicit pictures of children in the attachment, and has not seen them himself.

Has WILLIAMS committed an offence contrary to the Criminal Justice Act 1988, s. 160?

A Yes, because he downloaded images he knew would contain pornographic material, irrespective of his knowledge of its contents.

B Yes, because he has opened the attachment containing the pornographic images, irrespective of his knowledge of its contents.

C No, but only because he had not seen the images of the children.

D No, provided he had no cause to suspect it to be an indecent photograph of a child and he had not seen the images.

Question 7.27

Section 80 of the Sexual Offences Act 2003 outlines the notification requirements in relation to a sex act a person has committed.

In which of the following cases will the person *not* be liable to the notification requirements?

A They receive a two-year prison sentence.

B They are found not guilty by reason of insanity.

C They receive a caution for a sex offence in Scotland.

D They receive a conditional discharge.

Question 7.28

KENNERLEY meets a woman in a bar and asks her back to his house. He intends to have sexual intercourse with her, but believes she might resist so he puts sleeping tablets in her drink. The woman becomes drowsy and lies down on the sofa.

KENNERLEY goes over to her and takes hold of the belt on her jeans and moves her hips up and down in simulated sexual intercourse. At that moment his flatmate arrives home, KENNERLEY calls a taxi and puts the woman in it.

Which, if any, of the following offences, is KENNERLEY mostly likely to be charged with?

A An offence of attempted rape as he has administered drugs for that purpose.

B An offence of sexual assault by touching.

C An offence of causing a person to engage in sexual activity.

D No offence under the Sexual Offences Act, although possibly a common assault.

Question 7.29

HAMMAN is a GP in a health clinic and has been arrested and charged with several offences of sexual touching, contrary to s. 3 of the Sexual Offences Act 2003. Complaints have been made by several women that during examinations HAMMAN inserted a finger into their vaginas unnecessarily and that this was done to obtain sexual gratification. In interview, HAMMAN claimed that the touching was not at all sexual, and that it formed part of the examinations.

What would need to be shown by the prosecution, for HAMMAN's actions to fall within the definition of 'sexual', under s. 78 of the Sexual Offences Act 2003?

A That whatever HAMMAN's purpose, the actions were sexual, by their very nature.

B That HAMMAN received sexual gratification from the touching.

C That because of their nature the actions *may* be sexual and because of the circumstances or the purpose of any person in relation to them, they are sexual.

D That HAMMAN received sexual gratification from the touching and a reasonable person would consider the actions to be sexual.

ANSWERS

Answer 7.1

Answer **C** — The Sexual Offences Act 2003 still has consent as a key issue in rape. 'Consent' is defined by s. 74 as follows: 'For the purposes of this Part, a person consents if he agrees by choice, and has the freedom and capacity to make that choice.'

Sections 75 and 76 of the 2003 Act apply to rape, and s. 75 provides for presumptions that the person did not, in certain circumstances, consent *per se*:

(2) The circumstances are that —
    (a) any person was, at the time of the relevant act or immediately before it began, using violence against the complainant or causing the complainant to fear that immediate violence would be used against him;
    (b) any person was, at the time of the relevant act or immediately before it began, causing the complainant to fear that violence was being used, or that immediate violence would be used, against another person;
    (c) the complainant was, and the defendant was not, unlawfully detained at the time of the relevant act;
    (d) the complainant was asleep or otherwise unconscious at the time of the relevant act. . .

This means that as the girl was asleep when intercourse took place, and FERGUSON knew she was asleep, the complainant will be presumed not to have consented to the act and the defendant will be presumed not to have reasonably believed that the complainant consented.

Answer A is incorrect because, even though earlier consent was given, at the time of the act consent was presumed absent, even though the girl's condition was due to self-intoxication (which also makes answer B incorrect). This places an evidential burden upon the defendant, and not the prosecution, which makes answer D incorrect. The judge must be satisfied that the defendant can produce 'sufficient evidence' to justify putting the issue of consent before a jury; lack of such evidence will result in a direction to the jury to find the defendant guilty.

Crime, paras 1.10.3, 1.10.3.3

Answer 7.2

Answer **A** — Again this relates to consent, and s. 75(2)(f) states:

any person had administered to or caused to be taken by the complainant, without the complainant's consent, a substance which, having regard to when it was administered or taken, was capable of causing or enabling the complainant to be stupefied or over-powered at the time of the relevant act.

This being the case, and the accused knowing that it is the case, presumes lack of consent and the offence is made out. Note that rape now includes intentionally penetrating the mouth of another person. Assault by penetration does not include the mouth, and therefore answer B is incorrect. Administering a substance with intent is a preparatory offence, i.e. date rape drugs; once the sexual act is performed, rape is the appropriate charge and answer C is therefore incorrect. Causing a person to engage in sexual activity without consent requires some other person being forced into committing a sexual act (i.e. if JENKINSON had forced COLLINS to masturbate him), answer D is therefore incorrect.

Crime, paras 1.10.3, 1.10.3.3

Answer 7.3

Answer **D** — Section 66 of the 2003 Act makes it an offence for a person intentionally to expose his or her genitals where he or she intends that someone will see them and be caused alarm or distress. It requires more than simple public display, therefore answer A is incorrect; and it is not necessary for the defendant's genitals to have been seen by anyone, so answer B is therefore incorrect. Even had no one been caused alarm or distress, the offence would be made out with the relevant intention of the offender, so answer C is therefore incorrect.

Crime, para. 1.10.7.1

Answer 7.4

Answer **B** — Section 9 of the Sexual Offences Act 2003 makes it an offence for a person aged 18 or over intentionally to engage in sexual touching of a child under 16. Whether or not the child consented to the sexual activity is irrelevant, so answer C is therefore incorrect; but this is not the case in sexual assaults where lack of consent must be established, so answer A in therefore incorrect. 'Touching' is defined by s. 79(8) of the 2003 Act and basically covers all forms of physical contact, including penetration. You must also understand what is meant by 'sexual', and s. 78 defines it. Subsection (a) covers activity that the reasonable person would always consider to be sexual because of its nature; this may be sexual intercourse, but may also be masturbation. Subsection (b) covers activity that the reasonable person would consider, because of its nature, may or may not be sexual, depending on the circumstances, or the intentions of the person carrying it out or both: for example, digital penetration of the vagina may be sexual, or may be carried out for a medical reason. Provided the reasonable person views the activity as sexual then full intercourse does not have to be shown, so answer D is therefore incorrect.

Crime, para. 1.10.5.1

Answer 7.5

Answer **C** — Section 11 makes it an offence for a person aged 18 or over intentionally to engage in sexual activity when a child under 16 is present, or in a place from which he can be observed by the child, the purpose of which is for obtaining sexual gratification from the presence of the child. 'Sexual' is defined by s. 78. The offence is met where the child is under 16 years of age, therefore answer B is incorrect; and is committed by those who are aged 18 or over, therefore answer A is incorrect. The offence is committed even where the child apparently consents to watching the sexual act, and does not need to cause offence; answer D is therefore incorrect.

This offence is intended to cover the situation where someone seeks sexual gratification not from the sexual act itself, but rather from the fact that he is performing that act in the presence or intended presence of a child. The motive of sexual gratification is a necessary safeguard intended to avoid capturing those who engage in sexual activity in front of a child for a legitimate reason. For example, a teacher who sexually kisses his partner just outside the school gates could be deemed to be engaging in sexual activity intentionally in front of a child, and might otherwise be caught by the offence. Note that in the circumstances of the question an offence contrary to s. 13 of the 2003 Act would have been committed as the assailant was under 18, but you were asked specifically about s. 11.

Crime, para. 1.10.5.2

Answer 7.6

Answer **B** — Sections 30 to 33 of the Act deal with offences where the victim is unable to refuse to engage in or to watch a sexual activity because of, or for a reason related to, a mental disorder. It is a requirement of these offences that the offender knew, or could reasonably have been expected to know, that the victim had a mental disorder *and* that because of it he was likely to be unable to refuse. Note the *and*, which means that both elements of the offender's guilty knowledge have to be shown, therefore answer A is incorrect. Section 30 makes it an offence intentionally to touch someone sexually when that person, because of, or for a reason related to, a mental disorder is unable to refuse. The s. 78 definition of 'sexual' applies, and touching means all physical contact, including touching with any part of the body, with anything else and through anything, for example, through clothing. It includes penetration (s. 78(9)). Using inducements and/or threats and deceptions are separate offences in themselves (ss. 34 to 37) and are not requirements for this offence; answers C and D are therefore incorrect.

Crime, para. 1.10.6.2

Answer 7.7

Answer **C** — Section 1(1)(c) of the Protection of Children Act 1978 states:

(1) Subject to sections 1A and 1B, it is an offence for a person —
   (c) to have in his possession such indecent photographs or pseudo-photographs, with a view to their being distributed or shown by himself or others
   . . .

In these days of computer integration the storing and sharing of indecent images has attracted the attention of the courts as the law attempts to decipher the purpose that offenders have such images electronically stored. Note however that no specific intention to distribute is required, the requisite *mens rea* being 'a view to'; answer D is therefore incorrect.

Such IT issues were considered in *R v Dooley* [2005] EWCA Crim 3093 which mirrors the scenario of this question. The defendant maintained that he had intended to remove the pictures from the shared folder. The appeal turned on the judge's preliminary ruling on the meaning of 'with a view to' under s. 1(1)(c). The Court of Appeal agreed with the judge's ruling that there was a distinction between 'with the intention of' and 'with a view to' — where a defendant had knowledge that images were likely to be accessed by other people, any images would be downloaded 'with a view to distribute'. If one of the reasons the defendant left the pictures in the shared folder was so others could have access to them, he would be in possession of the images 'with a view to their being distributed'. However, as the court accepted that the defendant did not leave the pictures in the shared folder for that reason his conviction could not stand; answers A and B are therefore incorrect.

The court believed that 'with a view' to required more than the knowledge that the files could be accessed; as an analogy (although not a great one!) the court considered that 'a general may foresee the likelihood of his soldiers being killed in battle, but he surely does not send his troops into battle with a view to their being killed'.

Crime, para. 1.10.5.8

Answer 7.8

Answer **D** — The legislation states that a risk of sexual harm order (RSHO) may prohibit the defendant from doing anything which is necessary to protect a particular child, a group of children or children in general from sexual harm. It goes beyond a risk to any child or all of the children that go to the school, so answers A and B are therefore incorrect. Indeed, such an order can extend beyond the locality where the person is, so answer C is therefore incorrect. Although a RSHO can be made to protect a particular child or a group of children, it extends to children in general (provided they are under 16 years of age) who may be at risk of sexual harm from STEPHENSON.

Crime, para. 1.10.9.24

Answer 7.9

Answer **C** — Section 53 makes it an offence for a person intentionally to control another person's activities relating to prostitution, in any part of the world, where it is done for, or in the expectation of, gain for himself or a third party. Clearly YOUNG is controlling his girlfriend's activity, even although she is happy to go along with it, and it was done with a view to gain, therefore answer B is incorrect. 'Gain' is defined by s. 54 of the Act as any financial advantage, including the discharge of a debt or obligation to pay, or the provision of goods or services (including sexual services) for free, or at a discount. It also covers the goodwill of any person likely to bring such a financial advantage. So this would cover YOUNG inciting his girlfriend to work as a prostitute for DIBLEY, where YOUNG expects this will lead to DIBLEY providing him with cheap drugs at a later date. This future gain therefore makes answer A incorrect. It is immaterial that YOUNG will be in a household with extra income due to his girlfriend's 'activities'; the offence is complete with the goodwill, and answer D is therefore incorrect.

Crime, para. 1.10.10.2

Answer 7.10

Answer **C** — Although the threat was a deception, in that MARKS never intended hurting her husband, rape by deception relates to deception as to the purpose or the person, i.e. the defendant intentionally tells the complainant that digital penetration of her vagina is necessary for medical reasons when in fact it is for his sexual gratification, or where the defendant impersonates the complainant's partner, therefore answer B is incorrect. The husband would have to have been threatened with immediate violence, therefore answer A is incorrect. Also, s. 75 plainly states that the violence or threat can be against the complainant, or be threats of violence used against a person other than the complainant, therefore answer D is incorrect.

Crime, paras 1.10.3.3, 1.10.3.4

Answer 7.11

Answer **D** — Section 71 of the 2003 Act makes it an offence for a person to engage in sexual activity in a public lavatory. It is not necessary for anyone to have been alarmed or distressed by this activity, therefore answer A is incorrect. This offence can be committed by a male or female against a male or female, which is a change from the old offence of gross indecency, therefore answer B is incorrect. The definition of 'sexual' in s. 71 is idiosyncratic, as s. 71(2) states that 'for the purposes of this section, an activity is sexual if a reasonable person would, in all the circumstances but regardless of any person's purpose, consider it to be sexual'. The difference is that it is unlikely that the third party who witnesses the activity will have information about the purpose of the defendant. For this reason, the sexual activity is limited to that which a reasonable observer would see as unambiguously sexual. This is a wide definition, and includes more than just anal sex; answer C is therefore incorrect.

Crime, para. 1.10.7.3

Answer 7.12

Answer **D** — A person *can* dispute the caution, therefore answers A and B are incorrect. He or she must apply to the court within 14 days of the caution, therefore answer C is incorrect.

Crime, para. 1.10.10.4

Answer 7.13

Answer **B** — Sections 80 to 92 of the Sexual Offences Act 2003 re-enact, with amendments, Part 1 of the Sex Offenders Act 1997, which established a requirement on sex offenders to notify certain personal details to the police. This process is commonly known as 'registration', often referred to loosely as creating a 'sex offenders register'.

Section 84 sets out the requirements on a relevant offender to notify the police of changes to notified details. Under s. 84(1)(c), an offender must notify the police within 3 days, of the address of any premises he has stayed at within the UK, besides his home address, for a 'qualifying period'. This place might be a friend's or relative's house, or a hotel where he has stayed. A qualifying period is defined s. 84(6) as a period of 7 days, or 2 or more periods, in any 12 months, which taken together amount to 7 days. It is an accumulative period of 7 days, not 7 days straight, therefore answer A is incorrect; and for the same reason answer D is incorrect. It is not so exacting as to expect any change of address to be notified, therefore answer C is incorrect.

Crime, para. 1.10.9.5

Answer 7.14

Answer **A** — To prove the offence of kerb-crawling you have to show that the person solicited a woman either persistently, or in circumstances likely to cause annoyance. Although it can be committed from a motor vehicle, it must meet either of the two tests mentioned, so answer B is incorrect. On the subject of persistent soliciting, the prosecution must prove more than one act, i.e. separate approaches to more than one person, or two invitations to the same person. In essence, there must be a degree of repetition.

We now need to examine annoyance; it is sufficient if there was a likelihood of nuisance to other persons in the neighbourhood. BAKER's intention is of no consequence; answer D is therefore incorrect. In determining that likelihood, the character of the area is taken into account, e.g. how common is its use by prostitutes and its residential nature (*Paul* v *DPP* (1989) 90 Cr App R 173). Answer C is incorrect in that, even though the woman propositioned wasn't insulted, other people might have been; given that it is a residential area, this is more than likely. Ask yourself this: would the woman, or any other person in the area, have been annoyed had they known BAKER'S motives?

Crime, para. 1.10.10.4

Answer 7.15

Answer **D** — Section 48 makes it an offence for a person intentionally to cause or incite a child under 18 into prostitution or involvement in pornography in any part of the world. The prostitution or pornography itself does not need to take place for the offence to be committed. This offence is targeted at the recruitment into prostitution or pornography of a child who is not engaged in that activity at the time. The offence would be committed where a 'pimp' makes a living from the prostitution of others and encourages new recruits to work for him. It could also cover the situation where the defendant forces the victim to take part in child pornography for any reason.

Unlike the equivalent adult offence at s. 52, there is no requirement that the prostitution or pornography must be done for the gain of any of the persons involved, therefore KAREN'S mother is as culpable as the others. All three persons have incited the child, therefore answers A and B and C are incorrect.

Crime, para. 1.10.5.11

Answer 7.16

Answer **A** — There are two offences here. The first offence is under the Protection of Children Act 1978, of taking, making, distributing, showing, publishing, advertising and possessing with intent to distribute indecent photographs.

The second offence is committed under the Criminal Justice Act 1988, which added the offence of mere possession of such photography.

Therefore, offences would be committed in this scenario by the person distributing, PORTER, and the people possessing, both PORTER and WILLIS (answer B is incorrect).

The offence of distribution is to 'another person'; there is no requirement to distribute to more than one person (answer C is incorrect).

Distributing *will* include lending, which is why answer D is incorrect.

Crime, para. 1.10.5.8

Answer 7.17

Answer **A** — Section 39 makes it an offence for a care worker intentionally to cause or incite another person to engage in sexual activity when that person has a mental disorder and he is involved in his care. It will cover a range of behaviour, including the care worker causing or inciting the victim to have sexual intercourse with him, or causing or inciting the victim to masturbate a third person. The offence is committed if incitement takes place, even if sexual activity does not actually happen because, for example, a relative of the victim intervenes to prevent it. The Act goes on to define what is meant by 'care worker'; it is defined broadly to cover circumstances where a relationship exists because one person has a mental disorder and another person is regularly involved (or likely to be involved) face-to-face in their care, and that care arises from the mental disorder, whether on a primary or ancillary level, and whether on a paid or voluntary basis. It can include, for example, not only doctors, nurses and social workers, but also receptionists, cleaning staff, advocates or voluntary helpers. PAVETT *is* a care worker, therefore answers B and C are incorrect. Section 42(3) states *inter alia* that if the man is a patient for whom services are provided by a National Health Service body then he is included in this offence. The fact he is an outpatient is irrelevant; therefore answer D is incorrect.

Crime, para. 1.10.6.5

Answer 7.18

Answer **A** — There are two relevant offences where a person is premeditating a sexual offence. So what offence is intended? COLLINS clearly intends (although he may not realise it) to commit rape. Under the 2003 Act, rape differs from the offence in the Sexual Offences Act 1956, in that it requires that the defendant does not have a 'reasonable belief' in consent, rather than that he does not have an 'honest belief' in consent. COLLINS' belief is not reasonable, so he will commit rape; answer C is therefore incorrect.

There are two preparatory offences to consider: trespass with intent to commit sexual offence (s. 63); and committing an offence with intent to commit a sexual offence (s. 62). For an offence under s. 63, the person must be 'on any premises where he is a trespasser'. Whilst COLLINS is outside the bedroom window he is not a trespasser; answer B is therefore incorrect. When he breaks the window he has committed a criminal offence, and with the required intent an offence (s. 62) is committed regardless of whether or not the substantive sexual offence is committed; answer D is therefore incorrect.

Crime, paras 1.10.8.1, 1.10.8.2

Answer 7.19

Answer **D** — Section 15 makes it an offence for a person aged 18 or over to meet intentionally, or to travel with the intention of meeting, a child aged under 16 in any part of the world, if he has met or communicated with that child on at least two earlier occasions, and intends to commit a 'relevant offence' against that child either at the time of the meeting, or on a subsequent occasion. An offence is not committed if he reasonably believes the child to be 16 or over. The stumbling block to the offence in this question is the lack of a previous meeting. Had there been such previous meeting or communication then the offence would be complete as soon as WISE started travelling towards the meeting, and again when he actually does meet BEN. Note that simply arranging a meeting would not be captured by this offence; answer A is therefore incorrect. Because of the lack of two earlier communications, answers B and C are incorrect. The section is intended to cover situations where an adult establishes contact with a child through, for example, meetings, telephone conversations or communications on the Internet, and gains the child's trust and confidence so that he can arrange to meet the child for the purpose of committing a 'relevant offence' against the child ('relevant offences' are offences under Part 1 of this Act). The course of conduct prior to the meeting that triggers the offence may have an explicitly sexual content, such as entering into conversations with the child about the sexual acts he wants to engage in when they meet, or sending images of adult pornography. However, the prior meetings or communication need not have an explicitly sexual content and could, for example, simply involve giving the child swimming lessons or selling him sweets.

Crime, para. 1.10.5.4

Answer 7.20

Answer **B** — This offence mirrors that under s. 12 of causing a child to watch a sexual act, with the addition of the perpetrator being in a position of trust. There is a significant difference, however, in that for the abuse of position of trust offences, the child may be 16 or 17 (under 16 for the s. 12 offence); therefore answer C is incorrect. A position of trust is defined by s. 21 of the Act, and in relation to someone in education subsection (5) states:

> This subsection applies if A looks after persons under 18 who are receiving education at an educational institution and B is receiving, and A is not receiving, education at that institution.

'Receiving education at an educational institution' is defined by s. 22(4)(a) as:

> ...he is registered or otherwise enrolled as a pupil or student at the institution.

'Looks after persons under 18' is a wide caveat, which extends this section beyond the actual teacher/pupil relationship within a specific lesson; therefore answer A is incorrect.

Lastly, s. 12 outlines that it is an offence for a person aged 18 or over intentionally to cause a child, for the purposes of his own sexual gratification, to watch a third person engaging in sexual activity, or to look at an image of a person engaging in a sexual act. The act can be live or recorded, and there is no need for the child to be in close physical proximity to the sexual act. An example would be where he sends a child indecent images over the Internet. In order for an offence to be committed, the adult must act for his own sexual gratification. This ensures that adults showing children sex education material, either in a school or in another setting, will not be liable for this offence. However, this will not be an excuse if the act was done purely for sexual gratification. The term 'image' means a moving or still image, and includes an image produced by any means and, where the context permits, a three-dimensional image; therefore answer D is incorrect.

Crime, para. 1.10.5.5

Answer 7.21

Answer **D** — The offence of voyeurism is divided into three parts:

- The first offence involves a defendant observing another doing a private act with the relevant motive of gaining sexual gratification.
- The second offence deals with people operating equipment such as hoteliers or landlords using webcams to enable others to view live footage of their residents or tenants, in each case for the sexual gratification of those others.
- The third offence deals with the recording of the private act with the intention that the person doing the recording or another will look at the image and thereby obtain sexual gratification.

The three offences described above require proof that the victim does not consent to the observing, recording or operating of the relevant equipment for the purpose of the defendant or another's sexual gratification. The accused must know that the victim does not consent to his recording the act with that intention. It follows that consent to recording given by the victims for another purpose will not avail the accused; answers A and C are therefore incorrect.

A 'private act' is defined as where they are in a place which, in the circumstances, would reasonably be expected to provide privacy, and:

- their genitals, buttocks or breasts are exposed or covered only with underwear;

- they are using a lavatory; or
- they are doing a sexual act that is not of a kind ordinarily done in public.

So the fact that the persons could be seen in underwear makes this a 'private act' and within the scope of s. 67; answer B is therefore incorrect.

Crime, para. 1.10.7.2

Answer 7.22

Answer **A** — Section 87 of the Sexual Offences Act 2003 deals with the method of notification and related matters. It states:

(1) A person gives a notification under section 83(1), 84(1) or 85(1) by —
   (a) attending at such police station in his local police area as the Secretary of State may by regulations prescribe or, if there is more than one, at any of them, and
   (b) giving an oral notification to any police officer, or to any person authorised for the purpose by the officer in charge of the station.

The person must attend within the period of 3 days beginning with any change of his home address. The only option is personal attendance; answers B, C and D are therefore incorrect.

Crime, para. 1.10.9.8

Answer 7.23

Answer **D** — A Sexual Offences Prevention Order:

(a) prohibits the defendant from doing anything described in the order, and
(b) has effect for a fixed period (not less than 5 years) specified in the order or until further order (Sexual Offences Act 2003, s. 107(1)).

Such an order can cover any activity by the offender at all, whether that activity amounts to a criminal offence or a civil wrong, provided it is shown necessary for the purpose of protecting the public, or any particular members of the public, from serious sexual harm from the defendant. As it includes civil wrongs, answer A is incorrect.

A chief officer of police may by complaint to a magistrates' court apply for an order under this section in respect of a person who resides in his police area, or who the chief officer believes is in, or is intending to come to, his police area, if it appears to the chief officer that the person is a qualifying offender. A 'qualifying offender' is defined in s. 106(6) as a person who:

(a) has been convicted of an offence listed in Schedule 3 (other than at paragraph 60) or in Schedule 5,

(b) has been found not guilty of such an offence by reason of insanity,

(c) has been found to be under a disability and to have done the act charged against him in respect of such an offence, or

(d) in England and Wales or Northern Ireland, has been cautioned in respect of such an offence.

So the person does have to have previous convictions; therefore answers B and C are incorrect.

Crime, para. 1.10.9.16

Answer 7.24

Answer **D** — An offence is committed under s. 91 where the relevant person fails, without reasonable excuse, to comply with the notification requirements under the 2003 Act, the relevant person being the offender, and also the person who is subject to a parental direction; answer C is therefore incorrect. Under this direction the parent must ensure that the young offender attends at the police station with them when notification is being given. This does not mean that they can attend and give notification themselves, the person subject to the order must personally attend; answer B is therefore incorrect.

Reasonable excuse will be a question of fact for the court, but it is more than likely that given the circumstances of this case the parents will have such excuse, having done all they can to ensure attendance of their son, and will therefore not have committed the offence; answer A is therefore incorrect.

Crime, para. 1.10.9.17

Answer 7.25

Answer **C** — New legislation usually takes time to find precedents; given the amount in its predecessor it is not surprising that the Sexual Offences Act 2003 has already started!

The Court of Appeal in *R* v *H*, *The Times*, 8th February 2005 has held that the touching of an individual's clothing was sufficient to amount to 'touching' under s. 3; answers A and B are therefore incorrect.

It also confirmed that where touching was not by its nature 'sexual' it was appropriate to ask the jury to consider two questions:

- Would the jury, as twelve reasonable people, consider that the touching could be sexual?
- Whether the jury, as twelve reasonable people and in all the circumstances of the case, would consider that the purpose of the touching had in fact been sexual?

An affirmative answer to both questions led to a finding that the touching, in similar circumstances to this scenario, was sexual and the accused properly convicted. It is the circumstances of this scenario, or ROBINS' purpose in relation to it, that is important in what is 'sexual', not the victim's belief (which would be important, of course, but not definitive). A conviction could arise where the victim felt that the Act wasn't sexual applying the test in *H*; therefore answer D is incorrect.

Crime, para. 1.10.4.2

Answer 7.26

Answer **D** — Possession of indecent photographs of children is an offence contrary to the Criminal Justice Act 1988, s. 160.

Section 160 of the 1988 Act penalises possession, even though the possessor does not intend that the photograph or pseudo-photograph be distributed. Clearly WILLIAMS has the images in his possession.

However, a defendant has a defence to a charge under s. 160 if they can prove that they had a legitimate reason for having the photograph in their possession, or that they had not themselves seen the photograph, *and* neither knew nor had any reason to suspect that it was indecent, or that the photograph was sent to their without any prior request by them, and that they did not keep it for an unreasonable time.

A person who suspects that images in his possession are indecent but shows that he had no reason to suspect that they were images of children may rely on this statutory defence. So held the Court of Appeal in *R* v *Collier* [2004] EWCA Crim 1411.

Hooper LJ, in the reserved judgment of the court, said that the defence in s. 160(2)(b) would be made out if a defendant proved that he had not seen the indecent photograph of a child alleged in the charge against him *nor* had he had any cause to suspect it to be an indecent photograph of a child. Answer C is therefore incorrect. So, although knowing the general content of the attachment when downloading and opening it, not knowing its specific content permits the defence. Answers A and B are therefore incorrect.

Crime, para. 1.10.5.8

Answer 7.27

Answer **C** — The notification applies where:

- they are convicted of an offence listed in Schedule 3 — this covers most of the commonly occurring sex offences;
- they are found not guilty of such an offence by reason of insanity;
- they are found to be under a disability and to have done the act charged against them in respect of such an offence; or
- they are cautioned in respect of such an offence, not only in England and Wales but for an offence in Northern Ireland as well.

Note that a conviction is enough; no specific prison sentence needs to be imposed; answer A is therefore incorrect (don't forget you were asked which will *not* attract the requirements!). Those who are found guilty by reason of insanity and cautioned in England, Wales and Northern Ireland are subject to the requirements; therefore answer B is incorrect. However, as Scotland is not mentioned, the requirement does not extend to someone cautioned there; therefore answer C is *correct*.

The Court of Appeal has confirmed that conditional discharges count as 'convictions' and therefore those receiving such a punishment are subject to notification requirements (*R* v *Longworth* [2004] EWCA 2145); answer D is therefore incorrect.

Crime, para. 1.10.9.2

Answer 7.28

Answer **B** — The mental element in attempted rape is the same as that required for the full offence, namely intent to have sexual intercourse and the absence of reasonable belief in consent. It is not necessary to prove that the accused had gone so far as to attempt physical penetration of the vagina, anus or mouth. It suffices if acts be proved which the jury could regard as more than merely preparatory (*Attorney General's Reference (No. 1 of 1992)* [1993] 1 WLR 274). Clearly administering drugs in the circumstances outlined is preparatory, and indeed following the guidance of the *A G's Ref* above KENNERLEY would not have to go too much further to be guilty of attempted rape, as in *R* v *Gullefer* [1990] 1 WLR 1063, in which Lord Lane CJ stated that the crucial question was whether the accused had 'embarked upon the crime proper', but that it was not necessary that the accused should have reached a 'point of no return' in respect of the full offence. KENNERLEY has not and answer A is therefore incorrect.

An offence of causing a person to engage in sexual activity is committed where a person intentionally *causes* another person to engage in a sexual activity, i.e. a man forcing someone else to masturbate him. This is not the case here and answer C is therefore incorrect.

It is in fact sexual touching; in that KENNERLEY has intentionally 'touched' the woman, and by any reasonable person's view that touching is sexual. Although it is only her clothing he touched the Court of Appeal in *R v H, The Times*, 8 February 2005 has held that the touching of an individual's clothing was sufficient to amount to 'touching'; answer D is therefore incorrect.

Crime, para. 1.10.4.3

Answer 7.29

Answer **C** — Section 78 of the Sexual Offences Act 2003 provides that penetration, touching or any other activity will be sexual if a reasonable person would consider that:

(a) whatever its circumstances or any person's purpose in relation to it, it is sexual by its very nature; or
(b) because of its nature it *may* be sexual and because of its circumstances or the purpose of any person in relation to it, it is sexual.

Therefore, activity under (a) covers things that a reasonable person would always consider to be sexual (for example, masturbation). The activity under (b) above covers things that may or may not be considered sexual by a reasonable person depending on the circumstances or the intentions of the person carrying it out (or both). The example of a doctor inserting a finger into a vagina might be sexual under certain circumstances, but if done for a purely medical purpose in a hospital, it would not be. Since HAMMAN's actions would not always be considered sexual by their nature, answer A is incorrect.

If the activity would not appear to a reasonable person to be sexual, then it will not meet either criteria and, irrespective of any sexual gratification the person might derive from it, the activity will not be 'sexual'. Answers B and D are therefore incorrect.

Crime, paras 1.10.2.1, 1.10.4.2

8 | Child Protection

STUDY PREPARATION

It is important that officers recognise the significance of some victims particularly children and their vulnerabilities. Operational officers deal with situations involving these persons on a daily basis; it is important to recognise your powers.

Make sure you know the differences between the two offences under the Child Abduction Act 1984 (person connected and not connected to a child). The emotive issue of child cruelty is also covered here as well as legistation aimed directly at child protection, e.g. The Children Act 2004.

QUESTIONS

Question 8.1

JUAN was born in Spain but lives in the UK. He is separated from his wife, GAIL, and their four-year-old son, DAVID. GAIL had custody of DAVID and had refused to let JUAN take DAVID to see his grandparents in Spain. JUAN arranged for his brother to pick up DAVID from school one Friday and take him to Spain. He intended meeting them there, when he finished work later that evening. He knew GAIL would not consent, but intended to return DAVID at the end of the weekend.

In relation to offences that might have been committed under the Child Abduction Act 1984, which of the following is correct?

A Only JUAN is guilty of an offence; his brother is not 'connected with the child'.

B Only JUAN's brother is guilty of an offence; he physically took DAVID out of the UK.

C Both JUAN and his brother are guilty of offences in these circumstances.

D Neither person is guilty, as they intended to return DAVID to the UK.

Question 8.2

SHELLEY, aged 18, was a single parent, who had a baby aged 16 months. One winter, the baby developed a severe case of influenza, which resulted in hypothermia. Eventually the baby died. The baby had been ill for some time, and SHELLEY had not taken her to the doctor. SHELLEY was lawfully arrested for the offence of child cruelty, when she reported the death to the police.

What would the prosecution have to prove in order to convict SHELLEY of this offence?

A That her actions in denying medical care were wilful.
B That she was reckless in denying medical care to the child.
C That she intended to deny medical care to the child.
D That her denying medical care for the child included a positive act.

Question 8.3

Section 2 of the Child Abduction Act 1984 outlines the offence of child abduction, where the person is not connected to the child.

Who is the person entitled to lawful control of the child where the mother and father of the child in question were not married to each other at the time of the birth?

A Both mother and father.
B Either mother or father.
C Mother only.
D Mother and any person who reasonably believed he was the father.

Question 8.4

Section 1(2)(b) of the Children and Young Persons act 1933 provides that a person will have neglected a child who dies as a result of suffocation (not being suffocation caused by disease or the presence of any foreign body in the throat or air passages of the infant) whilst in bed with that child under the influence of drink. There are, however, restrictions on age to this offence.

What are those restrictions?

A The child must be under 2 and the person over 16.
B The child must be under 3 and the person over 16.
C The child must be under 3 and the person over 18.
D The child must be under 2 and the person over 18.

Question 8.5

FRANCES, aged 15, agreed to baby-sit her neighbours' two-year-old child, while her neighbours went out for the evening. During the evening, FRANCES's boyfriend rang her and asked if he could see her. FRANCES checked that the child was asleep, then slipped out of the house to meet her boyfriend. She had been gone from the house for about half an hour, when neighbours found the child wandering down the street in his pyjamas. The child was not injured during the incident.

In relation to the Children and Young Persons Act 1933, which of the following is correct?

A FRANCES has committed an offence of child cruelty through her neglect.

B FRANCES has committed an offence of child cruelty as her actions are wilful.

C FRANCES does not commit an offence of child cruelty in these circumstances.

D FRANCES does not commit an offence of child cruelty as the child was not injured.

Question 8.6

ROUSE had committed an offence against a child, and had a disqualification order imposed on him under the Criminal Justice and Court Services Act 2000 preventing unsuitable people from working with children. He is aware he is so disqualified. ROUSE was asked by a neighbour, FULLER, who runs an under-11 football team, if he was willing to be the kit manager. The only involvement ROUSE would have would be collecting the kit and washing it ready for the next game. ROUSE agrees to take on the post. FULLER is aware that ROUSE is so disqualified, but does not realise what this means.

In relation to applying for a position while disqualified contrary to s. 35 of the Criminal Justice and Court Services Act 2000 which of the following is correct?

A ROUSE does not commit the offence, as he did not *apply* for the position; he was *offered* and *accepted* it.

B ROUSE does not commit the offence as 'position' only relates to regulated positions not voluntary ones.

C ROUSE does commit the offence as he has accepted a voluntary position working with children. FULLER commits no offence.

D ROUSE does commit the offence as he has accepted a voluntary position, as does FULLER when she offered it.

Question 8.7

GALT was investigated by the police for ill-treating a child in a manner likely to cause unnecessary suffering or injury, so much so that the child actually died as a result.

Which of the following is correct?
A GALT may be charged with an offence only of child cruelty.
B GALT may be charged with an offence of child cruelty *and* homicide.
C GALT may be charged with an offence of child cruelty *or* homicide but not both.
D GALT may be charged with an offence only of homicide.

Question 8.8

LANGLEY has three children who are profoundly deaf; he himself suffers from Usher's Syndrome, which means that he has tunnel vision and night blindness. He is registered blind, and has been without a valid driving licence since it was withdrawn on medical grounds by the DVLA. LANGLEY regularly drove his children to school, and as such had been warned by social services that this must stop, and he had agreed it would. Two days later social services had information that LANGLEY had driven the children several hundred miles to be assessed by another school for deaf children. On learning what had happened, the family's social worker instructed the council's legal department to apply for an emergency protection order (EPO) pursuant to s. 44 of the Children Act 1989, which was granted. The police were informed and they intercepted the vehicle on the motorway being driven home with the children as passengers. The officers invoked their powers under s. 46 of the Children Act 1989 and took the children into police protection.

In relation to police action, which of the following is correct?
A The officers should not have invoked police protection whilst an EPO was in place.
B The police should only have invoked police protection whilst an EPO was in place where there are compelling reasons to do so.
C The police are entitled to invoke a police protection whilst an EPO was in place and this could never be unlawful.
D The police are entitled to invoke a police protection whilst an EPO was in place as the statutory scheme accords primacy to the EPO procedure.

Question 8.9

Section 46 of the Children Act 1989 deals with the protection of children in certain situations.

In relation to the section, which of the following statements is correct?
A A constable or social worker may remove a child to suitable accommodation.
B A constable in uniform may remove a child to suitable accommodation.
C A constable may only remove a child to a police station or hospital.
D A constable may remove a child to suitable accommodation.

Question 8.10

The Children Act 2004 provides that each children's services authority in England and Wales must make arrangements to promote co-operation between partner agencies, with a view to improving the wellbeing of children in the authority's area.

What age group are the authorities obliged to consider, when making such arrangements?
A Only children under 18.
B Generally children under 18, but may include in certain circumstances those of a maximum age of under 19.
C Generally children under 18, but may include in certain circumstances those of a maximum age of under 20.
D Generally children under 18, but may include in certain circumstances those of a maximum age of under 25.

Question 8.11

An 11-year-old child has been made subject of an emergency protection order under s. 44 of the Children Act 1989 taken out by social services and has been placed into temporary foster care. The child's father contacts her on her mobile phone and tells her that if she comes back to the family home she will be safe and taken away on a special holiday to see her grandmother who lives in France.

Has the father committed an offence of acting in contravention of a protection order?
A Yes, as the father has induced, assisted or incited the child to run away from foster care.
B Yes, as the father has induced, assisted or incited the child to run away from foster care and intends taking the child abroad.

C No, as the child wasn't directly in 'care' within the local authority area as foster care is not 'care' for the purposes of the legislation.

D No, as the offence would only be complete if the child actually leaves, or is taken away from the foster care by the father.

ANSWERS

Answer 8.1

Answer **C** — There are two offences under the Child Abduction Act 1984 that deal with taking a child under the age of 16.

Under s. 1 of the Act, an offence takes place where a person connected with a child under the age of 16 takes or sends the child out of the UK without the appropriate consent. This offence *may only be committed by a 'connected person'*; who will include the child's parent, father even if the parents are not married, the legal guardian, or a person with a residence order or lawful custody order.

As JUAN's brother does not fall within this group, he cannot commit this offence. However, to take DAVID lawfully out of the UK, JUAN would require the consent of the mother/guardian/person with a residence order or person with custody.

Obviously JUAN did not have consent to take DAVID out of the UK, and even though he did not actually take him, he committed the offence by sending him. Sending can include 'causing', or 'inducing', a child to go with another, which is why answer B is incorrect.

Under s. 2 of the Act, a person commits an offence if, without lawful authority or reasonable excuse, he takes or detains a child under the age of 16 so as to remove him from the lawful control of any person having lawful control of the child; or so as to keep him out of the lawful control of any person entitled to lawful control of the child (which would include GAIL). This offence may be committed by a person *who is not a 'connected person'*, and would be committed by the brother (which is why answer A is incorrect).

There is no requirement for the abduction to be permanent (making answer D incorrect).

Crime, paras 1.11.4.1, 1.11.4.2

Answer 8.2

Answer **A** — The circumstances in the question may amount to neglect, but the prosecution must prove that this was *wilful* (not reckless or intentional, which is why answers B and C are incorrect). The issue of *mens rea* was addressed in the case of *R* v *Sheppard* [1981] AC 394. Lord Diplock explained that:

...the jury must be satisfied (1) that the child did in fact need medical aid at the time at which the parent is charged with failing to provide it (the *actus reus*) and (2) either that the parent was aware at the time that the child's health might be at risk if it were not provided with medical aid, or that the parent's unawareness of this fact was due to his not caring whether the child's health was at risk or not (the *mens rea*).

There may be an element of 'objective recklessness' in the defendant's behaviour. However, the definition requires proof that a person was wilful in his or her actions.

Answer D is incorrect, as the offence can be committed either by an act, *or* by an omission.

Crime, para. 1.11.5

Answer 8.3

Answer **C** — The person entitled to lawful control of the child where the mother and father of the child in question were not married to each other at the time of the birth is the child's mother only (s. 2(2)(b)); answers A and B are therefore incorrect. If you went for D you may have been confused by s. 1(2), the definition of 'a person connected with a child'. The Child Abduction Act 1984, s. 1(2) states:

A person is connected with a child for the purposes of this section if —
(a) he is a parent of the child; or
(b) in the case of a child whose parents were not married to each other at the time of his birth, there are reasonable grounds for believing that he is the father of the child; or
(c) he is a guardian of the child; or
(d) he is a person in whose favour a residence order is in force with respect to the child; or
(e) he has custody of the child.

There is also a defence to a s. 2 offence which also recognises a person who reasonably believed he was the father of the child; but where they were not married, only the mother is the person entitled to lawful control, so answer D is therefore incorrect.

Crime, para. 1.11.4.1

Answer 8.4

Answer **B** — The Children and Young Persons Act 1933, s. 1(2) states:

(b) where it is proved that the death of an infant under three years of age was caused by suffocation (not being suffocation caused by disease or the presence of any foreign body in the throat or air passages of the infant) while the infant was in bed with some other person who has attained the age of sixteen years, that other person shall, if he was, when he went to bed, under the influence of drink, be deemed to have neglected the infant in a manner likely to cause injury to its health.

The child must be under 3 years of age and, like other aspects of this offence; the person must be at least 16 years of age; answers A, C and D are therefore incorrect.

Crime, para. 1.11.5

Answer 8.5

Answer **C** — To be guilty of an offence under the Children and Young Persons Act 1933, s. 1, an accused must have been over the age of 16 at the time of the offence, and must have 'had responsibility' for the child or young person in question. Although s. 1 creates just one offence, it may take a number of different forms. It may take the form of positive abuse (assault, ill-treatment, abandonment or exposure) or of mere neglect, or it may take the form of causing or procuring abuse or neglect. The abuse or neglect in question must be committed 'in a manner likely to cause unnecessary suffering or injury to health', but the offence is essentially a conduct crime rather than a result crime. It need not therefore be shown that any such injury was caused (answer D is therefore incorrect). FRANCES's actions may well have amounted to an offence under the Act, but she is outside the scope of the legislation by virtue of her age; answers A and B are therefore incorrect.

Crime, para. 1.11.5

Answer 8.6

Answer **D** — Section 35 states:

(1) An individual who is disqualified from working with children is guilty of an offence if he knowingly applies for, offers to do, accepts or does any work in a regulated position.

(2) An individual is guilty of an offence if he knowingly —
   (a) offers work in a regulated position to, or procures work in a regulated position for, an individual who is disqualified from working with children, or
   (b) fails to remove such an individual from such work.

(3) It is a defence for an individual charged with an offence under subsection (1) to prove that he did not know, and could not reasonably be expected to know, that he was disqualified from working with children.

There are two offences associated with being a disqualified person. The first offence arises where a disqualified person knowingly applies for, offers to do, accepts or does any work in a regulated position. Given the specific defence available (s. 35(2)), it would seem that the requirement of 'knowingly' here relates to the act of applying, offering or accepting work in a regulated position. Answer A is therefore incorrect. Regulated positions are generally those where the person's normal duties include working with children, whether in the public, private or voluntary sectors, and also in certain senior management roles such as social services and children's charities. Amongst the examples given by the Home Office is voluntary work at a children's football club. Answer B is therefore incorrect.

The second offence arises where a person offers or procures work in a regulated position for a person who is disqualified from working with children or fails to remove such an individual from that work This offence is clearly aimed at employers, though it would clearly extend beyond those circumstances and it does not have the statutory defence available. This seems slightly odd given that, of the two, a prospective employer is far less likely to know of the implications of a person's disqualification than the person disqualified. Therefore answer C is incorrect.

Crime, para. 1.11.3.1

Answer 8.7

Answer **B** — It is an offence of child cruelty when a person, in relation to a child:

wilfully assaults, ill-treats, neglects, abandons, or exposes him, or causes or procures him to be assaulted, ill-treated, neglected, abandoned, or exposed, in a manner likely to cause him unnecessary suffering or injury to health...

(Children and Young Persons Act 1933, s. 1).

A defendant may be charged with the above offence even where the child has died (see s. 1(3)(b)), but homicide should also be considered and both may be charged, particularly where intent is an issue. Consequently answers A, C and D are incorrect.

Crime, para. 1.11.5

Answer 8.8

Answer **B** — This scenario mirrors the case of *Langley* v *Liverpool City Council and Chief Constable of Merseyside* [2006] 1 WLR 375. In that case the police invoked their powers under s. 46 of the Children Act 1989 despite an EPO being in existence that the social services were going to raise when the children returned home.

The Court of Appeal considered the proper approach in these circumstances to be:

- there is no express provision in the Act prohibiting the police from invoking s. 46 where an EPO is in place and it is not desirable to imply a restriction which prohibits a constable from removing a child under s. 46 where he or she has reasonable cause to believe that the child would otherwise be likely to suffer significant harm; answer A is therefore incorrect;
- the s. 46 power to remove a child can therefore be exercised even where an EPO is in force in respect of the child;
- where a police officer knows that an EPO is in force, he/she should not exercise the power of removing a child under s. 46, unless there are compelling reasons to do so;
- the statutory scheme accords primacy to the EPO procedure under s. 44 because removal under that section is sanctioned by the court and involves a more elaborate, sophisticated and complete process of removal than under s. 46; answer D is therefore incorrect;
- consequently, the removal of children should usually be effected pursuant to an EPO, and s. 46 should only be invoked where it is not reasonably practicable to execute an EPO;
- in deciding whether it is practicable to execute an EPO, the police should always have regard to the paramount need to protect children from significant harm;
- failure to follow the statutory procedure may amount to the police officer's removal of the child under s. 46 being declared unlawful; answer C is therefore incorrect.

Crime, para. 1.11.6

Answer 8.9

Answer **D** — Section 46 states that where a constable has reasonable cause to believe that a child would otherwise be likely to suffer significant harm, he or she may remove that child to suitable accommodation and keep him or her there. Answer A is incorrect, as the section allows only a constable to remove the child (known as police protection). There is no requirement for the officer to be in uniform (answer B is therefore incorrect). The section does not specify that the child should only be taken to a police station or hospital (although these may be suitable places); the child may be taken to any suitable accommodation (which is why answer C is incorrect).

Crime, para. 1.11.6

Answer 8.10

Answer **D** — The general duties imposed on children's services authorities in England are set out in s. 10 of the Children Act 2004. The 'arrangements' required are to be made with a view to improving the well-being of children in the authority's area with regard to a number of aspects of children's well-being including:

- their physical and mental health and emotional well-being;
- protection from harm and neglect;
- their social and economic well-being;
- their education, training, recreation and the contribution made by them to society.

(s. 10(2)).

(Note that the parallel provisions with regard to Wales are found in s. 25).

The arrangements *may* include arrangements relating to people aged 18 or 19. However, in relevant cases, similar arrangements must be made for people *under the age of 25* if subject to s. 13 of the Learning and Skills Act 2000, (see s. 10(9)(c), or s. 25(10) in respect of children in Wales). Answers A, B and C are therefore incorrect.

Crime, para. 1.11.2.2

Answer 8.11

Answer **A** — Acting in contravention of protection order or power exercised under s. 46 of the Children Act 1989 (police protection power) is an offence contrary to s. 49 of the 1989 Act

The Children Act 1989, s. 49 states:

(1) A person shall be guilty of an offence if, knowingly and without lawful authority or reasonable excuse, he —
   (a) takes a child to whom this section applies away from the responsible person;
   (b) keeps such a child away from the responsible person; or
   (c) induces, assists or incites such a child to run away or stay away from the responsible person.

So the offence is complete when a person induces, assists or incites a child to run away, and doesn't necessarily involve actually taking the child away, although that action is also an offence under this section; answer D is therefore incorrect. In this section 'the responsible person' means any person who for the time being has care of him by virtue of the care order, the emergency protection order, or s. 46, as the case may be, this would include the foster carer; answer C is therefore incorrect.

8. Child Protection

The legislation does not mention an intention to take the child abroad, referring only to taking the child, or inducing the child to leave the place they were put if they were in care, subject to an EPO or police protection powers (s. 49(2)); answer B is therefore incorrect.

Crime, para. 1.11.6.2

9 | Offences Amounting to Dishonesty, Deception and Fraud

STUDY PREPARATION

To use the police vernacular, many subjects in this chapter are your 'bread and butter' offences. In the *Police Q&A Road Policing* book, we stress the importance of knowing basic definitions, in order to recognise the more complex offences. The same applies to many dishonesty offences. You simply cannot get away with not knowing the components that make up the definition of theft. Learning this will assist you with robbery, handling, burglary and aggravated burglary. Similarly, the concept of dishonesty is important to understanding — and proving — a number of offences.

Following on from this, you must be able to recognise the difference between the burglary offences under s. 9(1)(a) and s. 9(1)(b) of the Theft Act 1968, and when a person commits the aggravated offence, by having with them certain articles. Learning the definitions of robbery and handling will also be crucial, as well as the offences under s. 12 of the Act (taking and aggravated vehicle-taking).

There are other offences contained in the chapter that you may not come across regularly, such as abstracting electricity and blackmail. Deception offences are also important.

There is often an overlap between the various offences of deception; it is important to recognise the differences between each one. Practically, police officers are more likely to encounter deception where it arises from people obtaining property and services, as well as making off without payment. However, for completeness it is important to know all the offences, such as fraud, forgery, obtaining pecuniary advantage and evading liability.

QUESTIONS

Question 9.1

HARDING was in a shop with PERRY, who picked up a CD intending to steal it. PERRY realised he was being watched by SATO, a store detective, and placed the CD in HARDING'S pocket, without HARDING knowing. Before they left the store, HARDING realised what PERRY had done, and was about to put the CD back, but changed his mind and decided to keep it and try to leave without paying. On their way out, SATO stopped them.

Has HARDING committed an offence in these circumstances?

A No, as PERRY was the one who appropriated the property.

B Yes, he has committed the offence of theft in these circumstances.

C No, as he formed the intent to steal after appropriating the property.

D Yes, he has committed the offence of handling in these circumstances.

Question 9.2

MILLS was observed in a High Street store at the city centre to take three pairs of gloves from a display and leave without paying. She was observed by a plain-clothed police officer who happened to be at the store. He followed her outside and questioned her and arrested her, taking her to the nearest designated police station, where she was subsequently charged with theft. At no point was she obstructive or abusive to the police or to anyone else, and was fully cooperative to the investigation. When she was brought before the court the claimant pleaded guilty to theft. The court was told that she had numerous convictions of a similar kind. The prosecution wish to apply for an Anti-social Behaviour Order under s. 1(c) of the Crime and Disorder Act 1998 to prevent MILLS from entering retail stores in the city centre area.

In these circumstances can an Anti-social Behaviour Order be granted?

A Yes, such an order can be granted in all cases involving theft by shoplifting.

B Yes, as the defendant has numerous convictions of a similar kind.

C No, there was no evidence of anti-social behaviour by the defendant.

D No, such an order can never be granted in cases involving theft by shoplifting.

Question 9.3

HARVEY was walking past a post office, when he saw an elderly woman coming out. HARVEY produced a knife and threatened her, demanding she handed over her handbag. He had no intention of using the knife, but was trying to make the woman hand over her handbag. The woman was not scared and began hitting him with her bag until he eventually ran away.

Has HARVEY committed the offence of robbery in these circumstances?

A No, as the person was not put in fear of violence being used against her.
B Yes, as he intended to put her in fear of violence being used against her.
C No, but he could have committed attempted robbery.
D Yes, as he has committed attempted theft, using violence.

Question 9.4

LEWIS has had a dispute with his neighbour, PLATT. One night LEWIS got home from the pub, having had too much to drink, and found paint had been poured over his car. He was convinced that PLATT was responsible and so forced his way into PLATT'S house. LEWIS intended to beat PLATT up, causing really serious injury; however, he discovered the house was empty.

In relation to the offence of burglary (under s. 9 of the Theft Act 1968), which of the following is correct?

A An offence under s. 9(1)(b) has been committed even though no grievous bodily harm was caused.
B An offence under s. 9(1)(a) has not been committed as no grievous bodily harm was caused.
C An offence under s. 9(1)(a) has been committed even though no grievous bodily harm was caused.
D An offence under s. 9(1)(a) has not been committed as no assault or theft was carried out.

Question 9.5

PAUL and his family sold their house and bought a large camper van, which they kept permanently on a campsite. While they were out, MORRIS, tired from hitch-hiking, broke the door lock to sleep inside the van. Having fallen asleep on a bunk bed, MORRIS was woken up by the sound of children. He ran from the van grabbing some cans of food on the way out.

Which of the following is correct in relation to MORRIS?

A He has *not* committed burglary as a camper van is a vehicle, never a 'building'.

B He has committed burglary, under s. 9(1)(b), as a camper van is a 'building' here.

C He has committed burglary, under s. 9(1)(a), as a camper van is a 'building' here.

D He has *not* committed burglary, as the camper van was not occupied when he entered.

Question 9.6

BOURKE is in the rear garden of a large country house. He forces a ground floor window and enters, and when he enters his intention is to steal. As he is looking around for something to steal, he sees a samurai sword on display. The occupiers, who come in through the front door, disturb BOURKE and he picks up the sword to frighten them. BOURKE points the sword at the occupiers and threatens them with violence. Unafraid, the occupiers approach BOURKE, who drops the sword and runs out of the open front door.

At what stage, if at all, does BOURKE commit an offence of aggravated burglary?

A When he enters the house with intention to steal.

B When he picks up the sword with intention to threaten.

C When he points the sword at the occupiers with intention to threaten.

D No offence of aggravated burglary is committed in these circumstances.

Question 9.7

PARSONS asked his colleague JAMES if he could borrow her motor van to take his family on holiday for the weekend to West Wales. JAMES agreed; however, PARSONS had misled JAMES, and actually takes the motor van to a pop festival with some friends. He returns it in good condition at the end of the weekend.

Has PARSONS committed an offence (under s. 12 of the Theft Act 1968) of taking a vehicle without the owner's consent?

A Yes, he obtained JAMES' permission by deception.

B Yes, but only if the journey was further than the agreed destination.

C No, his deception did not negate the consent he obtained.

D Yes, unless he could show he believed JAMES would have consented.

Question 9.8

WEBB and LARTER were in a supermarket car park when they saw a car with the keys in the ignition. They decided to take the vehicle and WEBB got in the driver's seat; LARTER sat in the front passenger seat. While he was reversing out of the parking place, WEBB struck KANG, a shopper who was walking past. Both WEBB and LARTER got out of the car and ran off, leaving KANG behind with a bruised hip.

Has an offence been committed (under s. 12A of the Theft Act 1968) of aggravated vehicle-taking?

A No, the vehicle was not driven on a road.

B Yes, but only by WEBB, the driver.

C Only if it can be shown that the vehicle was driven dangerously.

D Yes, by both WEBB and LARTER.

Question 9.9

HOWELLS was working for a company that was going through financial difficulties, and as a result, he was laid off. One Friday evening, HOWELLS entered the company office through an insecure window. In order to cause financial hardship to the owners, he linked all the computers up to the Internet, intending that they should all stay on for the weekend.

Has HOWELLS committed the offence of abstracting electricity by his actions?

A Yes, the offence is complete in these circumstances.

B Yes, but a charge of burglary would be more appropriate.

C No, because he has not abstracted or diverted electricity.

D No, using a telephone would not amount to using electricity.

Question 9.10

TAYLOR and RUSSELL met one evening to discuss breaking into an electrical warehouse. It was agreed that TAYLOR would break in and hand the goods to RUSSELL outside in his van. They were joined by BIRCH, who agreed to keep the goods in his house for a few weeks, and MURPHY, who owned a second-hand store and would sell the goods. They agreed that the burglary would take place the following night.

Who, if anyone, has committed the offence of handling stolen goods in these circumstances?

A RUSSELL, BIRCH and MURPHY only.

B All four have committed the offence.
C Only BIRCH and MURPHY have committed the offence.
D None of these people has committed the offence.

Question 9.11

Section 22 of the Theft Act 1968 outlines the definition of 'goods' which may be handled.

Which of the following items will *not* be included in the definition of the offence of handling stolen goods?
A Goods that were stolen outside England and Wales.
B Goods obtained by deception and blackmail.
C Land belonging to another.
D An item that has been severed from the land by stealing.

Question 9.12

VINCENT applied for a job with a computer company. He falsely stated in his application form that he was proficient in using several computer packages, which were required by the company in the job description that was sent out with the application form. He was later interviewed, but was unsuccessful and did not get the job.

Has VINCENT committed an offence (under s. 16 of the Theft Act 1968) of obtaining a pecuniary advantage in these circumstances?
A Yes, even though he has not profited from his actions.
B No, because he has not made a financial gain.
C No, he has not received the opportunity to earn remuneration.
D Yes, he deceived the company into interviewing him.

Question 9.13

FRENCH and OSBORN went for a meal in their favourite restaurant, where they ate regularly. During the meal they consumed two bottles of wine each. For a laugh, at the end of the meal they both went to the toilet and climbed out of the window. They intended returning the next day to pay for the meal; however, the restaurant owner did not know this and called the police.

Have FRENCH and OSBORN committed an offence (under s. 3 of the Theft Act 1978) of making off without payment?

A Yes, but they would have a defence if they could show that they thought the owner would have consented in the circumstances.

B No, because they have not deceived the owner into thinking they would pay for the meals.

C No, they have not committed the offence in these circumstances as they intended returning to pay.

D Yes, they have committed the offence, regardless of their intention to pay, and would have no defence in the circumstances.

Question 9.14

GOMEZ was at his friend PETERS' flat and he had with him a stolen credit card, which he had recently used to obtain goods by deception. GOMEZ gave the card to PETERS, so that he could use it the next day. GOMEZ had no intention of using the card again.

Which of the following statements is true, in relation to s. 25 of the Theft Act 1968, regarding 'going equipped'?

A An offence has been committed by PETERS only, as GOMEZ did not intend using the card again.

B An offence has been committed by GOMEZ and PETERS in these circumstances.

C No offence has been committed by either PETERS or GOMEZ, as they were both in a dwelling.

D An offence has been committed by GOMEZ; PETERS commits no offence in these circumstances.

Question 9.15

GORDON fancied CLINTON, who worked with him. He asked her out during a Christmas party, but she refused as she was married. The following day, GORDON sent CLINTON an e-mail, stating that, unless she had sex with him, he was going to phone her husband and tell him they were having an affair.

Has GORDON committed the offence of blackmail in these circumstances?

A Yes, if it can be shown that CLINTON was in fear of the consequences.

B No, as GORDON was not seeking to gain or cause loss.

C Yes, as GORDON has made unwarranted demands with menace.

D No, the offence is committed only where a person demands money or other property.

Question 9.16

SCOTT was homeless and was sitting on a bench in the centre of his local town. He was sitting next to a bucket which had 'SAVE THE CHILDREN' written on it. Believing he was collecting money for charity, several people placed money in the bucket. SCOTT, who was trying to get money for food and not for charity, did not say anything at any time.

Has SCOTT committed an offence (under s. 15 of the Theft Act 1968) of obtaining property by deception?

A No, it cannot be shown that he used words to obtain property by deception.

B Yes, but only if it can be proved that he intended people to be deceived.

C Yes, but only if it can be shown that he was reckless as to whether people were deceived.

D No, he did not use any words or actions to obtain property by deception.

Question 9.17

GRANT is a member of a gym to which she took DUNCAN. At the gym there was a new person working in reception. GRANT showed her membership card to the receptionist, saying, 'She's a member, too, but she forgot her card'. DUNCAN was not a member, but said nothing and was allowed entry, without paying the usual fee for guests.

Who, if anyone, has committed an offence (under s. 1 of the Theft Act 1978) of obtaining a service by deception?

A Both have committed the offence in these circumstances.

B DUNCAN only; there is no offence of obtaining a service for another.

C Neither; the offence applies to a service that will be paid for in the future.

D Neither; they have committed the offence of evasion of liability under s. 2(1)(c) of the Theft Act.

Question 9.18

GORDON ordered some furniture from a second-hand shop. He paid a deposit and was due to pay the remainder on delivery. When the furniture arrived, GORDON gave the delivery driver a cheque, aware that it would not be honoured by the bank. However, he knew that he would have money in the relevant account in a month's time, and would be able to pay the bill then.

Has GORDON committed an offence (under s. 2(1)(b) of the Theft Act 1978) of evasion of liability by deception?

A Yes, but only if the shop owner decides to forgo the payment.
B No, as he does not intend to make a permanent default on the payment.
C Yes, he has made the shop owner wait for the money, which is an offence.
D No, the cheque represents payment, even if later it is not honoured.

Question 9.19

SHEWRING was a sales representative and was given a company mobile phone. According to company rules, employees had to pay for private telephone calls. At the end of each month, SHEWRING received a copy of the mobile phone bill and was required to highlight any private calls made and pay for them by cheque or cash. SHEWRING knew that the accounting department was always busy and the bills were never examined closely. As a result, SHEWRING regularly made international calls to family in America, but never declared these as private calls and never paid for them.

Could SHEWRING be found guilty of the offence of false accounting, under s. 17 of the Theft Act 1968?

A No, an offence under this section cannot be committed by an omission alone; there must be an act done by the accused.
B Yes, provided it can be shown that SHEWRING intended to permanently deprive the company of the money owed.
C Yes, an offence under this section may be committed by an omission alone.
D No, an offence under this section cannot be committed unless it is shown that documents were falsified, defaced or destroyed.

Question 9.20

CHANDLER is highly skilled in the forgery field, and produced a sophisticated set of plates from which he made a forged £20 note. Using a high specification laser copier, he photocopied a large quantity of these notes. Before releasing the notes, he spent some in local shops to test their quality.

Which elements of 'false instrument' would CHANDLER be guilty of in these circumstances?

A Making and using a false instrument.

B Copying and making a false instrument.

C Using a false instrument only.

D He is not guilty of any false instrument offence.

Question 9.21

GRAINGER is standing by a bus stop when his friend CARTER arrives in a motor vehicle and offers him a lift. Whilst the vehicle was stationary and switched off, GRAINGER notices that the ignition barrel of the vehicle has been damaged and suspects that the vehicle has been stolen. GRAINGER asks CARTER if the vehicle is stolen and CARTER says, 'What do you think?'. GRAINGER is still unsure whether the vehicle is stolen or not. CARTER goes to start the engine, but police officers arrive and arrest both GRAINGER and CARTER as the vehicle was taken without consent, although this was not by CARTER.

Has GRAINGER committed the offence under the Theft Act 1968, s. 12(1), of allowing himself to be carried?

A Yes, the fact he suspects the car to be stolen and his presence in it is enough — movement of the car is irrelevant.

B Yes, as the vehicle was actually taken without consent and GRAINGER suspects it was.

C No, as the vehicle did not actually move he cannot commit this offence — movement is essential.

D No, mere suspicion is not enough, GRAINGER must know the car is stolen — movement of the car is irrelevant.

Question 9.22

MILLIGAN commits a robbery and steals a mobile phone. He gives it to COMMONS, who works for a mobile telephone company, who alters the unique device identifier and sells the phone on to an unsuspecting buyer.

Considering the Mobile Telephones (Re-Programming) Act 2002, which of the following is true?

A This is an offence from the moment the phone is altered; there is no defence.

B This is an offence from the moment the phone is sold; there is no defence.

C This is an offence from the moment the phone is altered; there is a statutory defence however.

D This is an offence from the moment the phone is sold; there is a statutory defence however.

Question 9.23

KAPARSKI applies for a mortgage from a leading building society, who provide a free mortgage service. He falsely claims that he has a job and that he earns £20,000 per year. He provides accounts and testimonials, which are false, to obtain the mortgage. KAPARSKI hopes to be able to pay the monthly repayments, but this is unlikely given his unemployed status. The building society gives him the loan; however, they would not have done so if it had not been for his practised deception.

Which of the following is correct?

A KAPARSKI has obtained property by deception, as he deceived the building society.

B KAPARSKI has not committed any deception offence, there is no intention to permanently deprive.

C KAPARSKI has not obtained services by deception, as the mortgage service is provided free.

D KAPARSKI has committed an offence of obtaining services by deception.

Question 9.24

FRAMPTON visits his doctor in absolute agony due to a back injury. He demands an injection of a new wonder pain-killing drug, but as it is very expensive his doctor refuses and prescribes a strong pain-killer instead. Infuriated, FRAMPTON pulls a knife from his pocket and threatens to kill the doctor unless he gets the new drug; in fear for his life, the doctor gives him the injection. FRAMPTON apologises for his behaviour and leaves.

With respect to blackmail, which of the following is true.

A The offence is complete when the doctor gives FRAMPTON the injection.

B The offence is complete when FRAMPTON threatens the doctor.

C This is not blackmail as FRAMPTON has had no 'gain'.

D This is not blackmail as the doctor has had no loss, the drug belonging to the NHS.

Question 9.25

DIBLEY was employed by a company which had a charge account with a local service station for the purchase of petrol. DIBLEY was a regular visitor and was well known to HASTINGS, who worked as the petrol attendant. Due to staff restructuring DIBLEY was made redundant, and was no longer an employee of the company. DIBLEY is short of fuel and goes to the garage, where he fills the car with petrol. HASTINGS is the attendant and recognises DIBLEY; when told by DIBLEY to charge the petrol to the company's account, he does so.

In relation to obtaining property by deception, which of the following is correct?

A The offence is complete; he has operated a deception on the garage.

B The offence is complete; he has operated a deception on his former employers.

C The offence is not complete; the goods were obtained prior to the operated deception.

D The offence is not complete; the attendant was not deceived as to the identity of the driver.

Question 9.26

NICKLIN drove his van at the request of his friend to collect some copper wire, and he was surprised when he was directed to stop beside a large hedge. NICKLIN was even more surprised when his friend started to load up his van with the heavy-duty copper wire that was hidden below this bush, but not suspecting wrongdoing he assisted. On arrival at a local scrap yard he was even more surprised to be arrested by police officers investigating the theft of copper wire from an electrical power substation next to the hedge. The police, however, have no evidence that NICKLIN stole the wire, although he has numerous previous convictions for handling stolen goods. When questioned about the wire he said he had no knowledge that the goods were stolen, and that he 'asked no questions and was told no lies'.

In relation to a possible charge of handling stolen goods against NICKLIN which of the following is correct?

A He should be charged with both receiving/arranging to receive stolen goods and assisting/acting for the benefit of another.

B He should be charged with either receiving/arranging to receive stolen goods and assisting/acting for the benefit of another, but not both.

C He must be charged with receiving/arranging to receive stolen goods as it was obvious the goods were stolen.

D He should not be charged with any handling offence as he had no knowledge that the goods were stolen.

Question 9.27

Officers from the fraud squad are investigating HOLMES, who works as a bank employee, following a complaint from her employer. HOLMES is suspected of having dishonestly obtained a transfer of £10,000, by a deception, from the bank account of a customer into her own account. The officers have been unable to identify the account from which the money was taken. The investigation has revealed that only £5,000 was credited to HOLMES' own account and that this sum of money was transferred out immediately, to an unknown account. The investigating officers have been unable to trace the remaining £5,000, which they believe was transferred to another account also.

Ignoring any other offences that may have been committed, would the prosecution be able to prove a case against HOLMES for offences under s. 15A of the Theft Act 1968 (obtaining a money transfer by deception)?

A Yes, but only if the investigating officers can prove that HOLMES unlawfully retained some or all of the money.

B No, because the amount credited to HOLMES' account is less than the amount debited from the customer's account.

C Yes, in relation to the whole £10,000.

D No, unless they can identify the account from which the £10,000 was taken.

Question 9.28

KELLY had a large sum of money credited to his account from a mortgage lender. The police believed that this money transfer was made dishonestly and believe an offence contrary to s. 15A of the Theft Act 1968 has been perpetrated.

In ascertaining the causal connection between these accounts in relation to this offence, what needs to be established for an offence to be made out?

A Proof that a credit was made to his account dishonestly, do not need to prove debit from a particular account.

B Proof that a credit was made to his account dishonestly and debit from a particular account, which is identified.

C Proof that a credit was made to his account dishonestly and debit from a particular account, not necessarily identified.

D Proof that a debit from a particular account was made dishonestly, do not need to prove credit to his account.

Question 9.29

GRANGER worked in a petrol station owned by REECE. At the end of her shift one day she was told that her son had been in a car accident and was in hospital. GRANGER did not have a car and when she finished work, she took £10.00 from the till to pay for a taxi to take her to the hospital as she had no cash on her. In fact she had plenty of money in her bank account, but she didn't want to waste time by going to a cash point. GRANGER intended paying the money back the next day, thinking that REECE would not mind. REECE found that the till was short of money the next day and confronted GRANGER. REECE in reality did mind that the money had been taken and contacted the police to report a theft.

Would GRANGER be able to claim a defence to the offence of theft in these circumstances?

A No, because REECE in reality did not consent to the money being taken, and therefore it was theft.

B No, as she could have got her own money had she taken reasonable steps to get it.

C Yes, if she believed that REECE would have consented if he had known she was taking the money and the circumstances in which it was taken.

D Yes, if she believed that REECE would have consented if he had known she was taking the money.

Question 9.30

THOMPSON obtains several thousand pounds cash by stealing it from his elderly neighbour. THOMPSON deposits the cash in his own account but transfers it electronically to the bank account held by his friend EDWARDS, who is initially unaware of the transfer. A few days later EDWARDS discovers the money in his account, and when he asks where it came from, THOMPSON tells him the truth and EDWARDS agrees to keep it to assist THOMPSON.

At what point, if any, does he commit an offence of dishonestly retaining a wrongful credit contrary to the Theft Act 1968, s. 24A?

A He commits an offence under s. 24A as soon as the money is transferred into his account.

B He commits an offence under s. 24A as soon as he becomes aware that the money was stolen.

C He commits an offence under s. 24A as soon as he becomes aware that the money was stolen and fails to have it cancelled.

D He does not commit an offence contrary to s. 24A but will commit an offence of handling stolen goods as he assists in the retention of the funds.

ANSWERS

Answer 9.1

Answer **B** — A person commits theft if he or she dishonestly appropriates property belonging to another with the intention of permanently depriving the other of it (s. 1 of the Theft Act 1968).

Both people have 'appropriated' property in these circumstances, even though HARDING did so after he realised the property was in his pocket (therefore answer A is incorrect). Under s. 3(1), if having come by property (innocently or not) a person later assumes the rights of the owner, he or she commits theft (which is why answer C is incorrect). It is of no relevance that HARDING initially decided to return the property.

As the offence of handling will not be committed during the course of a theft, answer D is incorrect.

Crime, para. 1.12.2.3

Answer 9.2

Answer **C** — While there is no doubt that some thefts or acts of shoplifting can cause harassment, alarm or distress (particularly to those who lose a significant amount of their profit to such offences) and so fall within the provisions of the Crime and Disorder Act 1998, this criteria cannot be applied to all such offences, the Divisional Court so held in *R (On the Application of Mills)* v *Birmingham Magistrates' Court* [2005] EWHC 2732; answer A is therefore incorrect.

Therefore it is necessary to consider the individual facts of each case and an Anti-social Behaviour Order can be made where there is evidence of (well you guessed it!) anti-social behaviour and this applies equally to offences of theft; answer D is therefore incorrect. The fact that a person has numerous convictions of a similar kind will not be evidence of anti-social behaviour alone, and will not be grounds for the issuing of such an order; answer B is therefore incorrect.

Crime, para. 1.12.2

Answer 9.3

Answer **C** — To commit robbery, a person must steal and, immediately before or at the time of doing so and in order to do so, use force on any person, or put *or seek to put* a person in fear of being subjected to force then and there.

Answer B is incorrect, as HARVEY did not steal anything; therefore, he has not committed the full offence of robbery. He would be guilty of attempted robbery in these circumstances, as he sought to put the person in fear of being subjected to force (even though she was not actually scared — making answer A wrong). Further, whether or not he intended to use force is not relevant; his intent that the person should fear that he would is what counts in these circumstances. Lastly, the full offence of theft *must* take place. Therefore, answer D is incorrect.

Crime, para. 1.12.3

Answer 9.4

Answer **C** — A person who enters a building as a trespasser *with intent to inflict* grievous bodily harm commits an offence under s. 9(1)(a) of the Theft Act 1968 (therefore answer B is incorrect). In proving an intention to commit grievous bodily harm under s. 9(1)(a), it is not necessary to prove that an assault was actually committed (*Metropolitan Police Commissioner* v *Wilson* [1984] AC 242) and thus answer D is incorrect.

An offence was not committed under s. 9(1)(b), as a person must be shown to have inflicted grievous bodily harm under that section (answer A is therefore incorrect).

Crime, paras 1.12.4.1, 1.12.4.5

Answer 9.5

Answer **B** — Something will qualify as a 'building' if it has some degree of permanence. In *B and S* v *Leathley* [1979] Crim LR 314, the Crown Court held that the defendants had committed burglary. They had stolen some meat from a freezer container in a farmyard, which was considered to be permanently in place.

The meaning of 'building' is extended by s. 9(3), and includes an inhabited vehicle or vessel, and applies to any such vehicle or vessel at times when the person having a habitation in it is *not in residence as well as at times when he or she is*. (This makes both answers A and D incorrect.)

Answer C is incorrect because of the intention of the person when he entered the building. MORRIS entered intending to sleep (not one of the prerequisites of s. 9(1)(a)). MORRIS did, however, steal property, having entered as a trespasser, which makes him guilty of burglary under s. 9(1)(b).

Crime, para. 1.12.4.2

Answer 9.6

Answer **D** — Aggravated burglary is defined at s. 10 of the 1968 Act as follows:

> A person is guilty of aggravated burglary if he commits any burglary and at the time has with him any firearm or imitation firearm, any weapon of offence, or any explosive.

So, taking it logically, you must establish that the accused had any of the articles listed at the time he committed burglary, contrary either to s. 9(1)(a) or s. 9(1)(b). Certainly burglary is committed at the time BOURKE entered with the requisite intent, but he had no weapons, therefore answer A is incorrect.

If the burglary is under s. 9(1)(b), the offender must have one of the above articles with him when he commits the theft or grievous bodily warm. It is at that point in time that aggravated burglary is committed (and not at the time of entry). *R* v *O'Leary* (1986) 82 Cr App R 341. BOURKE commits no theft, as he leaves the sword behind him, and although an assault has probably taken place by threatening the occupiers with a sword, the injuries do not amount to grievous bodily warm; therefore answers B and C are incorrect. BOURKE has committed many offences in the scenario, but aggravated burglary is not one of them.

Crime, para. 1.12.5

Answer 9.7

Answer **C** — An offence under s. 12 is committed by a person who takes a vehicle without the owner's consent or other lawful authority, for his own or another's use.

The issue of consent was dealt with in the case of *R* v *Peart* [1970] 2 QB 672. The defendant was convicted of the offence, after he falsely represented to the owner of a car that he needed it to drive from Bedlington to Alnwick to sign a contract. The owner let him have the vehicle, provided he returned it that day. As he had intended all along, Peart drove the car instead to Burnley in the evening.

The Court of Appeal subsequently quashed Peart's conviction, by following the decision in *Whittaker* v *Campbell* [1984] QB 318, where it was held that *there is no general principle of law that fraud vitiates consent.*

Consequently, even if consent is obtained by fraud, it is still consent (making answer A incorrect). The case of *Peart* shows that even though the journey taken was different from the one agreed, an offence is still not committed (making answer B incorrect).

Lastly, the defence provided under s. 12(6) would apply *where an offence has been committed.* Since an offence has not been committed in these circumstances, the defence would not apply (which is why answer D is incorrect).

Crime, para. 1.12.7

Answer 9.8

Answer **D** — First, a person must commit an offence under s. 12(1) of the Theft Act 1968 either by taking the vehicle, *or* by being carried in it. Then, under s. 12A, it must be proved that at any time after the vehicle was taken (whether by him or another) and before it was recovered:

- it was driven dangerously on a road or public place; *or*
- owing to the driving of the vehicle, an accident occurred whereby injury was caused to any person; *or*
- owing to the driving of the vehicle, an accident occurred whereby damage was caused to any property other than the vehicle; *or*
- damage was caused to the vehicle.

The Act does not specify that the accident involving an injury to a person should occur on a road (making answer A incorrect).

All that the prosecution has to prove is that *one* of the circumstances above occurred before the car was recovered (*Dawes* v *DPP* (1995) 1 Cr App R 65) (answer C is incorrect for this reason).

Answer A is incorrect because the offence may be committed by either the driver or the passenger, provided one of the circumstances apply.

Crime, paras 1.12.7, 1.12.8

Answer 9.9

Answer **A** — Under s. 13 of the Theft Act 1968, a person who dishonestly uses, without due authority, or dishonestly causes to be *wasted or diverted*, any electricity, shall be guilty of an offence.

As electricity is not 'property', a specific offence was created to deal with its dishonest use or waste. For this reason electricity cannot be 'stolen', and therefore its dishonest use or wastage cannot form an element of burglary (making answer B incorrect).

Diverting a domestic electrical supply so as to bypass the meter, or using another's telephone without authority (*Low* v *Blease* [1975] Crim LR 513) would be examples of this offence, as would unauthorised surfing on the Internet by an employee at work, provided in each case that dishonesty was present (making answers C and D incorrect).

Crime, para. 1.12.10

Answer 9.10

Answer **D** — Quite simply, there can be no offence under s. 22 of the Theft Act 1968, unless goods have been stolen (answers A and B are therefore incorrect). Even though two of the participants have arranged to receive stolen goods, they will not commit the offence until the burglary takes place (answer C is therefore also incorrect).

If the plan ever does come to fruition, TAYLOR, as the person stealing the goods, would not commit the offence. It is debatable whether RUSSELL would do so, if he assisted with the burglary, as he might be guilty of that offence.

Crime, para. 1.12.11

Answer 9.11

Answer **C** — A person *can* be convicted of handling if the goods were stolen outside England and Wales, but only if the goods were taken in circumstances which amounted to an offence in the other country. Goods obtained by deception and blackmail *are* included in the definition of handling. Goods will include money and every other description of property *except* land, and includes things severed from the land by stealing (s. 34(2)(b) of the Theft Act 1968).

The items included in answers A, B and D *are* included in the definition of 'goods' that can be handled under s. 22 of the Theft Act 1968. The only *incorrect* answer is C — if you selected this one, you will be correct!

Crime, paras 1.12.11, 1.12.11.1

Answer 9.12

Answer **C** — A person who by any deception dishonestly obtains for himself any pecuniary advantage commits an offence. A pecuniary advantage may be obtained when trying to borrow from an overdraft, taking out a policy of insurance, or when given the opportunity to earn remuneration or greater remuneration in employment (or betting).

In the circumstances given, VINCENT has not obtained the opportunity to earn remuneration, as he was not been given the job. (Although an attempt to commit the offence may be present, answer D is therefore incorrect.)

There is no requirement for a person to actually profit from his or her deception; therefore, if he had been successful with his application, answer A would have been correct. Answer B is incorrect in any circumstances.

Crime, para. 1.13.3

Answer 9.13

Answer **C** — This is a typical question where police officers would think practically and decide, 'I would arrest those, where it was necessary to do so'. Avoid this approach and answer questions purely as points of law.

A person commits an offence under s. 3 of the Theft Act 1978 if, knowing that payment on the spot for goods supplied or services received is required, he or she dishonestly makes off without paying *with intent to avoid payment*.

In the scenario, even though the couple have made off without paying, there is no offence if they intend to defer payment to a later date (even though morally their actions may be regarded as wrong!) (Answer D is therefore incorrect.)

There is no requirement that the person practised some deception to prove the offence; simply making off with the required intent is enough (which is why answer B is incorrect).

The defence in answer A has been made up and does not exist.

Crime, para. 1.12.15

Answer 9.14

Answer **D** — A person commits an offence under s. 25 of the Theft Act 1968 when, not at his place of abode, he has with him any article for use in the course of or in connection with any burglary, theft or cheat (cheat includes deception).

The offence is designed as a preventative measure and therefore cannot be committed by a deed done in the past. The offence will be committed by a person who has an article with him or her for use by *someone else* (*R* v *Ellames* [1974] 3 All ER 130).

Applying the Act to this scenario, GOMEZ was not at his place of abode and had with him a credit card, which he intended PETERS to use in the future in a cheat (offence committed, even though he had no intention of using it again, which is why answer A is incorrect).

The card was given to PETERS and, although he intended using it, he *was* at his place of abode. Consequently, no offence is committed until PETERS leaves his house, and therefore answer B is incorrect.

Answer C is incorrect because the offence may be committed by a person in a dwelling — provided it is not the place where he or she lives!

Crime, para. 1.12.14

Answer 9.15

Answer **B** — Blackmail is committed when a person, with a view to gain for himself or another, or with intent to cause loss to another, makes any unwarranted demands with menaces (s. 21 of the Theft Act 1968).

Under s. 34 of the Act, 'gain' and 'loss' mean to gain or lose in money or other property. It will not apply where a person is making demands for sexual favours. Consequently, answers A, C and D are incorrect.

Crime, para. 1.12.16

Answer 9.16

Answer **C** — The prosecution would have to show that SCOTT either intended people to believe he was collecting money for charity, *or* that he was reckless to that fact (making B incorrect). The reckless element is subjective, although the prosecution would have to show that the defendant at least gave some thought to his conduct (*R* v *Goldman* [1997] Crim LR 894).

Conduct can include *omissions* (*R* v *Shama* [1990] 1 WLR 661); therefore, the fact that the person did not say or do anything would not provide a defence (which is why answers A and D are incorrect).

Crime, paras 1.13.1, 1.13.1.1

Answer 9.17

Answer **A** — A deception occurs where a person has induced another to confer a benefit by doing some act, or causing or permitting some act to be done, on the understanding that a benefit *has been or will* be paid for (therefore answer C is incorrect).

The Court of Appeal has accepted that obtaining a service for another will amount to an offence under s. 1 of the Theft Act 1978 (*R* v *Nathan* [1997] Crim LR 835), making answer B incorrect.

Evasion of liability is dealt with later in the chapter, but the circumstances outlined do not constitute an offence under s. 2(1)(c), as there is no provision under the section in respect of obtaining an abatement of liability *for another* (therefore answer D is incorrect).

Crime, para. 1.13.4

Answer 9.18

Answer **B** — A person commits an offence under s. 2(1)(b) of the Theft Act 1978 if, with intent to make *permanent default* in whole or in part on any existing liability to make a payment, or with intent to let another do so, he or she dishonestly induces the creditor or any person claiming payment on behalf of the creditor to wait for payment (whether or not the due date for payment is deferred) or to forgo payment.

Even though he has made the shop owner wait for the money, it would have to be shown that GORDON intended *permanently* to default on the payment (for example, if GORDON changed address after presenting the cheque), which is why answer C is incorrect.

Unlike the other two offences in s. 2(1), it is not necessary under s. 2(1)(b) to show that the person to whom the money was owed decided to forgo all or part of the payment (making answer A incorrect).

Answer D is incorrect because s. 2(3) of the Act states:

> For purposes of subsection (1)(b) a person induced to take in payment a cheque or other security for money by way of conditional satisfaction of a pre-existing liability is to be treated *not* as being paid but as being induced to wait for payment.

Crime, para. 1.13.5

Answer 9.19

Answer **C** — Section 17 of the Theft Act 1968 creates *two* offences: destroying, defacing, falsifying etc. accounts and documents (s. 17(1)(a)); and using false or misleading accounts or documents in furnishing information (s. 17(1)(b)). An offence under s. 17 can be committed by omission as well as by an act. Failing to make an entry in an accounts book, altering a till receipt or supplying an auditor with records that are incomplete may, if accompanied by the other ingredients, amount to an offence. In *R* v *Shama* [1990] 1 WLR 661 the Court of Appeal upheld the conviction of a telephone operator who had failed even to start filling out standard forms provided by his employer for the recording of international calls. He was held to have falsified the forms by leaving them unmarked (see Blackstone's Criminal Practice 2005). Answers A and D are therefore incorrect.

Unlike the offence of theft there is no requirement to prove an intention permanently to deprive — but there is a need to show dishonesty on behalf of the accused. Answer B is therefore incorrect.

Crime, para. 1.13.7.1

Answer 9.20

Answer **D** — Quite simply, offences classed as forgery include virtually every kind of document *except* bank notes. Therefore, as he has been involved in 'forging' bank notes, CHANDLER cannot commit the offences of making and using a false instrument (answer A is incorrect), copying and making a false instrument (answer B is incorrect) and using a false instrument (answer C is incorrect). Offences relating to currency are dealt with by the Forgery and Counterfeiting Act 1981.

Crime, para. 1.13.7.4

Answer 9.21

Answer **C** — On a charge of driving or allowing himself to be carried in or on a conveyance taken without authority, it must be proved that the accused knew that the conveyance had been taken without lawful authority (*R v Diggin* (1980) 72 Cr App R 204, *Boldizsar v Knight* [1980] Crim LR 653); therefore, answers A and B are incorrect. However, it seems that the accused need not be aware that the taker took the conveyance for his own or another's use.

It is also not enough for the prosecution to prove that the accused was in or on the conveyance. There must have been some movement of the conveyance (*R v Miller* [1976] Crim LR 417; also see *Diggin*). If a taker of a motor vehicle offers a person a lift and he gets into the seat next to the driver, the person is not allowing himself to be driven before the driver turns on the ignition switch (*Diggin*).

So answer D is almost correct. However, it is essential that a conveyance be moved in order for it to be taken, however small that movement may be, and this is the same even though the accused is only allowing himself to be carried. Answer D is therefore incorrect.

Crime, para. 1.12.7.3

Answer 9.22

Answer **C** — This offence was created to try to prevent the increasing criminal activity involving mobile handsets. The offence is committed where the unique identifier is either changed or interfered with, and is not reliant on a future sale of the phone; answers B and D are therefore incorrect. There is, however, a statutory defence, exclusive to manufacturers or those with written consent of the manufacturers; answer A is therefore incorrect.

Crime, para. 1.12.11.7

Answer 9.23

Answer **D** — On a charge of obtaining property by deception contrary to the Theft Act 1968, s. 15(1), the prosecution must prove that the accused acted dishonestly and with the intention of permanently depriving another of the property. As to intention permanently to deprive, the whole of the definition of this concept in the Theft Act 1968, s. 6, is applicable to s. 15 by virtue of s. 15(3). In this question, the accused does not have such intention; answer A is therefore incorrect.

The Theft Act 1978, s. 1(2), defines 'services' in terms of benefits (which would include accommodation, travel, education, medical care, etc.), but excludes benefits which are provided gratuitously. In *R v Halai* [1983] Crim LR 624, the Court of Appeal held that a building society had not provided services merely by allowing the accused to open a savings account because building societies do not charge any fees for such accounts. The position would be different if the accused practices his deception in order to open a current account with a bank which charges for services provided to such accounts (*R v Shortland* [1995] Crim LR 893). It was also held in *Halai* that a mortgage advance falls outside the definition of 'services'. This ruling was widely criticised (and seems downright daft), but has been captured by the Theft Act 1978, s. 1(3), which was inserted by the Theft (Amendment) Act 1996, s. 4. This puts the situation of obtaining a loan by deception squarely within the offence of obtaining services; answers B and C are therefore incorrect.

Crime, paras 1.13.2, 1.13.4.1

Answer 9.24

Answer **B** — The points to prove for an offence of blackmail are:

- with a view to gain;
- for self or another; *or*
- with intent to cause loss to another;
- made an unwarranted demand with menaces.

Using a knife to threaten to kill someone is most certainly an unwarranted demand ('unwarranted demand' is defined as an unreasonable or unfair demand) and menacing! 'Menaces' is loosely delineated as threat (including a veiled one) of any action detrimental or unpleasant to the person addressed. And the offence is complete at the time the demand is made, not when its desired consequences are brought about; answer A is therefore incorrect.

As the demand must be made with a view to the person's gain, has FRAMP-TON actually 'gained'? The gain must be in money or other property and can be temporary or permanent. In a case not mentioned in the manual, it was held that the drug was property and the injection involved 'gain' to the accused as he achieved pain relief. The fact that it was injected into him rather than being handed over did not mean that FRAMPTON did not gain that property; answer C is incorrect. There does not have to be a loss, provided the demand is made with a view to gain; answer D is therefore incorrect.

Crime, para. 1.12.16.1

Answer 9.25

Answer **C** — Where a deceit is practised after the goods are obtained, there will be no operating deception, which is a prerequisite for a s. 15 offence. So although DIBLEY has deceived the garage, as the deceit occurred after he obtained the goods, the most appropriate charge would be theft; answer A is thus incorrect. Similar principles are found in the 1978 Act. If, for example, the accused has paid a hotelier with a stolen cheque for services already provided, this cannot in itself amount to an offence under the Theft Act 1978, s. 1, because the services have already been obtained (*R* v *Collis-Smith* [1971] Crim LR 716). In *R* v *Coady* [1996] Crim LR 518, where the accused acted in a manner similar to this question, it was held that a deception must operate on the victim (who must be human, therefore answer B is incorrect) before ownership of the property is passed to the offender. In *Coady* the accused's conviction was quashed because the trial judge had failed to warn the jury of the requirement that the deception must have been operating on the attendant before the petrol was obtained. The deception relates to the practice, not the identity, of the defendant; answer D is therefore incorrect.

Crime, paras 1.13.1.1, 1.13.2

Answer 9.26

Answer **A** — Although generally speaking a charge should specify exactly what it is the person is actually accused of, and that where alternatives exist, to charge both would be bad for duplicity, handling stolen goods is a case in contrast.

In *R* v *Nicklin* [1977] 1 WLR 403 the accused was charged with handling stolen property by dishonestly receiving it, knowing or believing it to be stolen, contrary to s. 22(1) of the Theft Act 1968. The defendant pleaded not guilty to that charge but accepted that he had assisted in the removal of the stolen property (the circumstances mirror the scenario of this question). He was found guilty of handling stolen goods and dishonestly assisting in the removal or disposing of them for the benefit of [another] knowing or believing the same to have been stolen. He appealed (understandably) that he had been convicted of an offence that he wasn't even charged with!

His appeal was allowed and the conviction quashed, the Court of Appeal stated *per curiam* that a conviction of a particular type of handling can be upheld where the indictment simply alleges the offence of handling and the generalised form has led to no injustice or confusion; but the better practice is to particularise the form of handling for which the defendant is blamed. If there is any uncertainty about which form of handling two counts will generally cover every form; one count for the first limb of s. 22(1) of the Theft Act 1968, dishonestly receiving, and a second count for the second limb, dishonestly undertaking or assisting in the retention, removal, disposal or realisation or arranging to do those things.

It is not bad for duplicity to charge both strands of the offence therefore; answer B is therefore incorrect. In this scenario to charge only one strand would be wrong, following *Nicklin* a conviction would not be forthcoming; answer C is therefore incorrect.

You must show that the defendant knew or believed the goods to be stolen. Mere suspicion, however strong, will not be enough (*R* v *Griffiths* (1974) 60 Cr App R 14). Deliberate 'blindness' to the true identity of the goods would suffice but the distinction is a fine one in practice. It can be very difficult to prove knowledge or belief on the part of, say, a second-hand dealer who 'asks no questions'. Because there are practical difficulties in proving the required *mens rea*, s. 27(3) of the 1968 Act makes special provision to allow evidence of the defendant's previous convictions, or previous recent involvement with stolen goods, to be admitted; in these circumstances there would be more than enough evidence to charge the defendant, not to charge would be erroneous and therefore answer D is incorrect.

Crime, para. 1.12.11.4

Answer 9.27

Answer **C** — The Theft Act 1968, s. 15A(1) states that a person is guilty of an offence if by any deception he dishonestly obtains a money transfer for himself or another. Under s. 15A(2), a money transfer occurs when —

(a) a debit is made to one account,
(b) a credit is made to another, and
(c) the credit results from the debit or the debit results from the credit.

Under s. 15A(4)(a), it is immaterial (in particular) whether the amount credited is the same as the amount debited. Answer B is therefore incorrect.

It is not necessary to identify which particular account has been debited, providing that there was a debiting of *an account,* which was causally connected with the credit (see *Holmes* v *Governor of Brixton Prison* [2005] 1 All ER 490). Answer D is therefore incorrect.

Lastly, there is a specific offence, under s. 24A of the Act, of dishonestly retaining a wrongful credit. However, this is a separate offence from s. 15A, which does not require the prosecution to prove that the defendant 'retained' any credit. The offence is made out when the transfer is made, together with the element of dishonesty. Answer A is therefore incorrect.

Crime, para. 1.13.6.1

Answer 9.28

Answer **C** — An offence contrary to s. 15A of the Theft Act 1968 requires a credit made to a bank account, a debit made to another account and a direct causal connection between the two (proof that the credit was as a direct result of the debit, i.e. the money debited from account A dishonestly was the money credited to account B). Answers A and D are therefore incorrect.

It is not necessary, however, to identify which particular account has been debited provided that there was a debiting of *an account,* which was causally connected with the credit (*Holmes* v *Governor of Brixton Prison* [2005] 1 All ER 490). Answer B is therefore incorrect.

Crime, para. 1.13.6.1

Answer 9.29

Answer **C** — Under s. 2(1)(b) of the Theft Act 1968, a person's appropriation of property belonging to another is not to be regarded as dishonest if he/she appropriates the property in the belief that he/she would have the other's consent if the other knew of the appropriation **and** the circumstances of it. Therefore, the person appropriating the property must believe both elements, i.e. that the other person would have consented had he/she known of the appropriation and the circumstances of it. Answer D is therefore incorrect.

It is the belief of the person appropriating the property that is important, regardless of the belief of the owner. Therefore, even though REECE would state that he did not consent to the money being taken, if GRANGER can convince the court of the above two elements, she may have a defence. Answer A is therefore incorrect. This includes occasions where the defendant had access to other funds, which could have been obtained by taking reasonable steps as this directly relates to the circumstances under which the defendant took the money, i.e. urgency in attending at the hospital; answer B is therefore incorrect.

Crime, para. 1.12.2.1

Answer 9.30

Answer **C** — One consequence of the decision of the House of Lords in *R* v *Preddy* [1996] AC 815 is that, where a person dishonestly obtains a money transfer from another the sum thereby credited to the first person's account can no longer be categorised as stolen goods. This indeed was the view of the Law Commission when reviewing the impact of *Preddy*. Furthermore, even where a person, A, pays stolen bank notes directly into his account, the proceeds of a subsequent transfer from that account to an account held by another person B cannot be classed as stolen goods, because any credit balance thereby created in B's account is an entirely different chose ('thing in action') from the credit balance which previously represented the stolen money in A's account. B's credit balance admittedly represents the proceeds of A's original crime, but it has never done so in the hands of the original thief, and any argument that it does so in the hands of a handler of the stolen property (i.e. B) is circular, because that presupposes the very point it seeks to establish, namely that the funds in B's account are stolen goods! As they are not 'stolen goods' and therefore cannot be 'handled'; answer D is therefore incorrect.

The Theft Act 1968, s. 24A addresses this problem in three ways.

First, s. 24A(3) deals with cases in which a wrongful credit is made to the accused's account as a result of a s. 15A Theft Act offence (here a person is guilty of an offence if by any deception he dishonestly obtains a money transfer for himself or another.). Where the accused was himself responsible for the s. 15A offence, there would be no point in charging him with a s. 24A offence as well, but there may be cases in which it is easier to prove that he became aware of the wrongful credit rather than he was actually involved in obtaining the credit himself.

Secondly, s. 24A(4) broadens the scope of s. 24A to cases in which the accused dishonestly retains a credit which he knows or correctly believes derives from an offence of:

- theft;
- blackmail;
- a s. 15A offence; or
- stolen goods.

If, for example, A pays stolen money into his account and transfers the funds from that account to an account owned by B, a wrongful credit has been made to B's account, and B may commit a s. 24A offence if he dishonestly retains it, knowing or believing it to be derived from one or other of those offences. In this scenario this is exactly what happened, and the s. 24A offence is complete only when the defendant dishonestly retained it; answers A and B are therefore incorrect.

Lastly, s. 24A(8) provides that any money dishonestly withdrawn from an account to which a wrongful credit has been made can be classed once again as stolen goods.

It is curious that the proceeds of A's original theft can be classed as stolen goods when paid into A's own bank account, yet cease to be stolen goods when effectively 'transferred' to B's account, and yet revert to being stolen goods when dishonestly withdrawn as cash by B; but that is the law.

Any volunteers for a transfer to fraud investigation?

Crime, para. 1.12.17

STUDY PREPARATION

The definition of criminal damage needs attention in the first instance, and you will have to know the various components, such as lawful excuse, protection, recklessness, damage, property and belonging to another. In addition to these statutory issues there are many decided cases on each of these points.

It is important to learn the basic definition, before turning to the aggravated offences. Each one of these is similar to the other, with the defendant's intent being of key significance.

It is also worth paying attention to contamination of goods. Although the offences associated with the definition are reasonably long and complicated, this is an area that may receive considerable further attention in the current climate of terrorist threats.

QUESTIONS

Question 10.1

PETERS lived in the countryside and was having trouble with a fox, which had attacked her cat. One day she managed to corner the fox in her neighbour's field, but it escaped into a hole. PETERS set fire to the grass surrounding the hole, but unfortunately the fire spread to her neighbour's shed. When the fire was eventually extinguished, they found that the fox had been killed, as well as two of the farmer's chickens and some wild geese that he had tamed some time before.

Given that PETERS may be guilty of reckless criminal damage to property (the shed), would she also be guilty of criminal damage to any of the animals?

A Yes, to the chickens only.

B Yes, to the chickens and the geese.

C No, as animals are not property.

D Yes, to all three animals.

Question 10.2

POWERS and WARNE were in the centre of their local town. It had been snowing and they decided to have a snowball fight. POWERS made a snowball and threw it at WARNE, who ducked. The snowball smashed through a nearby shop window. POWERS was arrested, but says in his interview that he had not realised that any damage would be caused.

What must the prosecution prove in order to show that he had been reckless?

A That the risk of damage to the window was obvious and POWERS should have seen that risk.

B That the risk of damage to the window would have been obvious to a reasonably intelligent person and that POWERS ignored that risk.

C That the risk of damage to the window would have been obvious to POWERS if he had stopped to think about it.

D That the risk of damage to some property was foreseen by POWERS and he went on to take that risk.

Question 10.3

SINGH worked in a car park. While at work on a very hot day, he was told about a dog that was locked in one of the cars, with the windows closed. SINGH went to the car and saw the dog lying on the back seat. He thought that the dog was suffering and, believing that the owner would have consented, he smashed the window. As he was doing this, the owner of the car, MORGAN, returned. It appeared that the dog had not been there long, and it was asleep. MORGAN accused SINGH of causing criminal damage.

In relation to the defence under s. 5(2)(a) of the Criminal Damage Act 1971 (belief that he had consent to the damage to the property in question) only, which of the following statements is correct?

A SINGH could claim this defence if he could show that a reasonable person would have consented to the damage.

B SINGH could claim this defence if he believed that MORGAN would have consented, had she known the circumstances.

C SINGH could *not* claim this defence as he was reckless in these circumstances.

D SINGH could *not* claim this defence as MORGAN, knowing the circumstances, would not have consented.

Question 10.4

When proving an offence under s. 1(2) of the Criminal Damage Act 1971 (aggravated criminal damage), *mens rea* must be shown.

In which of the following circumstances is the offence made out?

A The person intended to cause criminal damage and intended to endanger a person's life.

B The person intended or was reckless as to whether damage would be caused, and intended or was reckless as to whether life would be endangered.

C The person intended or was reckless as to whether a person's life would be endangered.

D The person intended to cause criminal damage only, and was reckless as to whether a person's life would be endangered.

Question 10.5

The Anti-social Behaviour Act, s. 54 makes it an offence to sell aerosol paint to certain people.

To which of the following people would it be illegal to sell aerosol paint?

A Someone who is 16 years of age or under.

B Someone who is or appears to be 16 years of age or under.

C Someone who is under 16 years of age.

D Someone who is or appears to be under 16 years of age.

Question 10.6

Criminal damage under s. 2 of the Criminal Damage Act 1971 is an offence of intent.

When considering an offence under s. 2 (threats to destroy or damage property) what must the prosecution prove?

A That the accused intended that the victim would fear that the damage would be carried out immediately.

B That the accused intended to cause damage and intended to induce fear that damage would be carried out.

C That the accused intended that the victim would fear that the damage would be carried out.

D That the victim did in fact fear that the accused would carry out the threat to cause damage.

Question 10.7

WILKINS and MARTIN are members of an extreme animal rights group. MARTIN applied for a job in a zoo, and they planned that if he was successful, he would damage customers' cars by placing sharp tacks under the tyres. WILKINS bought ten packets of tacks at a DIY store the day before MARTIN's interview, intending to give them to him if he got the job.

Has either person committed an offence under s. 3 of the Criminal Damage Act 1971 (having articles with intent to damage property)?

A Only WILKINS; he has control of the articles, intending that MARTIN should use them to cause damage.

B Neither person, as WILKINS does not intend to use the articles himself to cause criminal damage.

C Both people, because of their joint intent that MARTIN should use the articles to cause damage.

D Neither person, as the intent to commit damage is conditional on MARTIN being successful in his interview.

Question 10.8

THATCHER works in a butcher's shop. As a joke, on 1 April he came in early and sprinkled icing sugar on some meat on display. He then left a note for his boss, claiming to be from an animal rights group, saying they had sprinkled rat poison on the food. Unfortunately, before he was able to stop him, his boss threw the meat away.

Has THATCHER committed an offence under s. 38 of the Public Order Act 1986 (contamination of goods)?

A Yes, because he has caused economic loss to his employer.

B No, because he has not caused public alarm or anxiety.

C No, because he has not actually contaminated any goods.

D No, because he only intended his employer to treat it as a joke.

Question 10.9

Section 2 of the Criminal Damage Act 1971 makes it an offence, in certain circumstances, to threaten to damage or destroy your own property.

Which of the following is true in relation to this offence?

A It is an offence to threaten to damage your own property regardless of the circumstances.

B It is an offence to threaten to damage your own property, but only where there is danger to your own or any other person's life.

C It is an offence to threaten to damage your own property, but only where there is danger to any other person's life.

D It is an offence to threaten to damage your own property under *any* circumstances.

Question 10.10

McFARLANE went to a local kebab shop following a night out with his friends. Having purchased a kebab he feared he had been overcharged and asked for a refund, which was refused. The owner of the kebab shop then asked him to leave or the police would be called. Grudgingly McFARLANE went outside and walked away; after about 20 yards he kicked a parked car and was heard to say 'bloody immigrants' as he did so, the car was damaged. The owner of the kebab shop was in fact not an immigrant, having been born in England and the car did not belong to him.

Has McFARLANE committed racially aggravated criminal damage?

A This is racially aggravated criminal damage as the offence committed was aggravated by racism.

B This is racially aggravated criminal damage as the hostility shown was based on the shop owner's membership or presumed membership of a racial or religious group.

C This is not racially aggravated criminal damage as the offence committed was not aggravated by racism, merely accompanied by it.

D This is not racially aggravated criminal damage as the victim was not the subject of the membership or presumed membership of a racial or religious group.

Question 10.11

FIAK was arrested for an offence of being in charge of a motor vehicle whilst over the prescribed limit, and following a reading that showed he was well over the prescribed limit he was placed in a cell and detained. FIAK was angry that in his view he had not been properly given his rights, and so he put the blanket he had been given down the toilet and flushed it until the cell floor was flooded. As a result of his actions the cell had to be closed until it had been cleaned, and the blanket had to be sent to be cleaned and dried.

In relation to a possible charge of criminal damage in relation to FIAK's actions, which of the following is correct?

A It would only be criminal damage to the blanket should the toilet have contained urine or faeces when it was put down there.

B It would only be criminal damage to the cell as that had to be taken out of service and was out of commission.

C It would be criminal damage in relation to both as the blanket could not be used until it had been dried out and the flooded cell remained out of action until the water was cleared.

D It would not be criminal damage in either case as both would dry, and when dry they would return to their original state.

Question 10.12

VENNERS has been charged with an offence of arson, contrary to s. 1(3) of the Criminal Damage Act 1971. It is alleged that VENNERS set fire to a car belonging to a neighbour because of a long-standing dispute. The fire endangered no one, as it occurred in the middle of the night, away from any dwelling houses. The car was completely written off and the insurance company have placed its value as £3,500.

Which of the following statements is correct, in relation to where VENNERS should be tried for this offence?

A Because the value of the damage was under £5,000, the case should be tried in the magistrates' court.

B Because it involved arson, the case should be tried in the Crown Court.

C Because no life was endangered, the case should be tried in the magistrates' court.

D Because the value of the damage was over £2,000, the case should be tried in the Crown Court.

ANSWERS

Answer 10.1

Answer **B** — Section 10 of the Criminal Damage Act 1971 describes 'property' as:

> ... property of a tangible nature, whether real or personal, including money and —
> (a) including wild creatures which have been tamed or are ordinarily kept in captivity ...

Quite simply, the geese have been tamed and are therefore 'property'. Likewise, the chickens are ordinarily kept in captivity and are therefore 'property'. The fox is not 'property', as it is neither tamed, nor ordinarily kept in captivity. Consequently, answers A, C and D are incorrect.

Crime, para. 1.14.2.3

Answer 10.2

Answer **D** — What is important now to the concept of recklessness (since the House of Lords considered it in *R* v *G & R* [2003] 3 WLR 1060) is that the defendant had foreseen the risk yet gone on to take it. Their Lordships held that a person acts recklessly (in a criminal damage case) where:

- With respect to a *circumstance*, he or she is aware of a risk that existed or would exist.
- With respect to a *result or consequence*, he or she is aware of a risk that it would occur and it is, in the circumstances known to him or her, unreasonable to take the risk.

It is more than the risk being obvious to the offender; he or she must then go on to take that risk with such knowledge: answers A and C are therefore incorrect. The previous case law held that a 'reasonable person' test existed for the risk. This has been overturned by *R & G* and the test now sits squarely with the offender's knowledge of the risk, and his or her willingness to take that risk; answer B is therefore incorrect.

Crime, para. 1.14.2.8

Answer 10.3

Answer **B** — A person shall be treated as having lawful excuse under s. 5(2) of the Criminal Damage Act 1971:

(a) if at the time of the act or acts alleged to constitute the offence he believed that the person or persons whom he believed to be entitled to consent to the destruction of or damage to the property in question had so consented, or would have so consented to it if he or they had known of the destruction or damage and its circumstances...

Provided a person holds a genuine, reasonably held belief that the owner of the property would have consented had they known the circumstances, he or she will not be guilty of an offence. (It must be based on the defendant's own belief, not that of a reasonable person or the owner of the property, making answers A and D incorrect.)

SINGH is not guilty of recklessness; he intended to break the window (making C incorrect).

Crime, para. 1.14.2.6

Answer 10.4

Answer **B** — A person is guilty of an offence under s. 1(2) of the Criminal Damage Act 1971, if they damage/destroy property intending *or* reckless as to whether damage is caused to their own property, or another's, *and* they intend *or* are reckless as to whether a person's life is endangered.

Either the elements of intent *or* recklessness must be proved in relation to both the damage and the endangerment to life for this offence to be made out. All four answers are fairly similar, but only answer B contains all the elements required to prove the offence. Consequently, answers A, C and D are incorrect.

Please note the change in the concept of recklessness brought about by the decision of the House of Lords in *R* v *G & R* [2003] 3 WLR 1060.

Crime, para. 1.14.3

Answer 10.5

Answer **C** — A person commits the offence by selling the aerosol to a person under 16 years of age. There is a defence courtesy of s. 4, for the person who reasonable believes the person was not under the age of 16 and took all reasonable steps to determine the purchaser's age. The section makes no mention of the apparent age of the purchaser; answers A, C and D are incorrect.

Crime, para. 1.14.7

Answer 10.6

Answer **C** — This is an offence of intention; that is, the key element is the *defendant's intention* that the person receiving the threat fears it would be carried out.

The s. 2 offence under the Criminal Damage Act 1971, which originates from the need to tackle protection racketeers, is very straightforward: there is no need to show that the other person actually feared or even believed that the threat would be carried out (making answer D incorrect).

Also, there is no need to show that the defendant intended to carry out the threat; nor does it matter whether the threat was even capable of being carried out (which is why answer B is incorrect).

Answers A and C are similar; however, C is correct because there is no requirement to show that the accused intended to cause fear of *immediate* damage.

Crime, para. 1.14.5

Answer 10.7

Answer **A** — Section 3 of the Criminal Damage Act 1971 states:

> A person who has anything in his custody or under his control, intending without lawful excuse to use it or cause or permit another to use it —
> (a) to destroy or damage any property belonging to some other person; or
> (b) to destroy or damage his own or the user's property in a way which he knows is likely to endanger the life of some other person;
> shall be guilty of an offence.

Answer B is incorrect, as a person may have control of articles which he or she intends to permit another to use. Answer C is incorrect, as MARTIN did not have the articles in his custody or control at any time.

Answer D is incorrect because a conditional intention to use an article if given circumstances arise will amount to an offence (*R* v *Buckingham* (1976) 63 Cr App R 159).

Crime, para. 1.14.6

Answer 10.8

Answer **D** — Under s. 38 of the Public Order Act 1986, it is necessary to prove that a person contaminated or interfered with goods, or made it appear that goods have been contaminated or interfered with, or threatened or claimed to have done so.

However, the person must have done so *with the intention* of causing public alarm or anxiety, or of causing injury to members of the public consuming or using the goods, or of causing economic loss to any person by reason of the goods being shunned by members of the public, or of causing economic loss to any person by reason of steps taken to avoid such alarm or anxiety, injury or loss.

Therefore, even though THATCHER in the circumstances may have contaminated goods, and even caused economic loss, he did not do so with the required intention and cannot be guilty of this offence. (Answer A is therefore incorrect.)

Had THATCHER been proved to have had the required intent, answers B and C would still be incorrect, because there is no need to prove a person actually caused public alarm/anxiety, and the offence may be committed without actually contaminating goods.

Crime, para. 1.14.8

Answer 10.9

Answer **C** — The Criminal Damage Act 1971, s. 2(b) states it is an offence for a person to threaten:

> (b) to destroy or damage his own property in a way which he knows is likely to endanger the life of that other or a third person;

So you can threaten to damage your own property, but it is only an offence where another's life is in danger. Consequently answers A, B and D are incorrect.

Crime, para. 1.14.5

Answer 10.10

Answer **D** — For simple criminal damage to be racially or religiously aggravated the circumstances as set out at s. 28(1)(a) of the Crime and Disorder Act 1998 apply, namely that the defendant demonstrates hostility towards the victim:

- at the time of, or
- immediately before or after

committing the offence, and that hostility is based on the victim's membership or presumed membership of a racial or religious group. The courts have shown that they are prepared to adopt a wide approach when interpreting this important legislation, however not wide enough to incorporate where the hostility is towards someone other than the actual victim of the offence. In this scenario the hostility was shown towards the kebab shop owner, however he was not the owner of the car and ultimately not the victim of criminal damage; answers A and B are therefore incorrect.

In *R* v *Rogers* [2005] EWCA Crim 2863 the Court of Appeal considered whether verbal abuse towards three Spanish women on the grounds of their being 'foreigners' constituted abuse towards a racial group under the Crime and Disorder Act 1998, s. 28(4). The Court agreed it was, however it noted that the very wide meaning of racial group under s. 28(4) gives rise to a danger of aggravated offences being charged where mere 'vulgar abuse' had included racial epithets that did not truly indicate hostility to the race in question. Consequently, s. 28 should not be used unless the prosecuting authority is satisfied that the facts truly suggest that the offence was aggravated (rather than simply accompanied) by racism. This is a fine line, and police officers may have difficulty in distinguishing between the two; in this scenario had the car belonged to the shop owner would the defendant's actions have been seen to be aggravated by racism or merely accompanied by racism? Thankfully on this occasion the distinction does not have to be made as the owner was not in fact the victim of the offence; and for this reason answer C is incorrect.

Crime, para. 1.14.2.1

Answer 10.11

Answer **C** — Although a key feature of the Criminal Damage Act 1971, strangely enough the terms 'destroy' or 'damage' are not defined. The courts have often been left to muse over what is and what is not 'damaged', and have taken an eclectic view when interpreting these terms. 'Destroying' property would suggest that it has been rendered useless, but there is no need to prove that 'damage' to property is in any way permanent or irreparable.

The Concise Oxford Dictionary explains damage as 'harm or injury impairing the value or usefulness of something . . .'. In *Morphitis* v *Salmon* [1990] Crim LR 48, the transcript of Auld J's judgment reads:

> The authorities show that the term 'damage' for the purpose of this provision, should be widely interpreted so as to conclude not only permanent or temporary physical harm, but also permanent or temporary impairment of value or usefulness.

This view was endorsed in *R* v *Fiak* [2005] EWCA Crim 2381; in that case the defendant had been arrested and placed in a police cell which he flooded by stuffing a blanket down the cell lavatory and repeatedly flushing. The defendant argued that there was no evidence that the blanket or the cell had been 'damaged'; the water had been clean and both the blanket and the cell could be used again when dry.

This argument of course assumes the absence of any possible contamination or infection from the lavatory itself, and the confident expectation that there would be none (how many police cell toilets would this apply to!). The Court of Appeal disagreed and held that, while the effect of the defendant's actions in relation to the blanket and the cell was remediable, the reality was that the blanket could not be used until it had been dried and the flooded cell was out of action until the water had been cleared. Therefore both had sustained damage for the purposes of the Act; answers A, B and D are therefore incorrect.

Crime, para. 1.14.2.2

Answer 10.12

Answer **B** — Section s. 1(3) of the Criminal Damage Act 1971 states that an offence committed under this section by destroying or damaging property by fire shall be charged as arson. The offence of criminal damage is triable either way, but if the value of the property destroyed or the damage done is less than £5,000, the offence is to be tried summarily (s. 22 of the Magistrates' Courts Act 1980). It follows that if the value of the damage is greater than £5,000, the offence is to be tried on indictment (this figure was previously £2,000).

However, if the damage in such a case was caused by fire (arson), s. 22 of the Magistrates' Courts Act 1980 will not apply, and the case must be tried on indictment and answers A and D are incorrect. This rule will apply even if the fire does not endanger life; therefore answer C is incorrect.

Crime, para. 1.14.2

11 Offences Against the Administration of Justice and Public Interest

STUDY PREPARATION

This chapter tests your knowledge of those offences which exist to deter people from interfering with the proper course of justice. Included in this chapter are questions relating to perjury, false statements contempt of court and corruption. The common law offence of perverting the course of justice is included, as are the statutory offences of intimidating witnesses and jurors. Particular crimes relating to those who assist offenders by protecting or hiding them are tested, as are those relating to wasting police time — an area that may also come into greater use as pressures on police resources intensify.

QUESTIONS

Question 11.1

DAVIDSON is giving evidence in court in his own defence. He is not religious and has taken the affirmation instead of swearing on the Bible. The evidence he gives is that he was not at the scene of the offence, stating he was elsewhere. This is in fact untrue and DAVIDSON knows it.

Has DAVIDSON committed perjury?

A   No, perjury cannot be committed by a defendant.
B   No, perjury can only be committed by a 'sworn' witness.
C   Yes, provided it is shown he intended to mislead the court.
D   Yes, he has given false testimony and knows it to be false.

Question 11.2

BOWDITCH has committed a summary offence. Constable SOUTHALL is making enquiries into the whereabouts of BOWDITCH and goes to BOWDITCH's sister's house to see if he is there. BOWDITCH is in fact in the house, and his sister knows he is. BOWDITCH has told her that he committed the offence. Constable SOUTHALL asks the sister if she has seen BOWDITCH. She says she hasn't and that he has gone to his cousin's home in Manchester. Having no reason to disbelieve her, the officer leaves, intending to pursue the matter with Greater Manchester Police.

Which of the following statements is true?
A The sister has committed an offence of assisting an offender.
B The sister has committed an offence of harbouring an offender.
C The sister has not committed an offence of assisting an offender.
D The sister has committed no offence.

Question 11.3

BOWDEN is the local authority building works manager. Aware that his girlfriend has just moved into a new, rather dilapidated house, BOWDEN arranges for a team of workers from the council to go to her house and do some work. They use materials that were meant for council premises and they do the work in council time.

Considering corruption offences, which, if any, offence has BOWDEN committed?
A Common law corruption.
B Public bodies corruption.
C Corruption of agents.
D He has not committed any offence of corruption.

Question 11.4

SUTTON makes a mobile telephone call to his neighbour stating that a child has just fallen into the river and been swept downstream. His neighbour calls the police and a search commences. Several officers are involved, and the force air support unit is called in to assist. Later SUTTON admits he made the incident up as he had received a speeding ticket last week. In total 25 police hours were wasted and the cost came to £21,000.

Which of the following statements is true?
A SUTTON is guilty of wasting police time as the limit of 21 hours has been passed.

B SUTTON is guilty of wasting police time as he falsely raised fears for the safety of a person.

C SUTTON is not guilty of wasting police time as he did not contact the police himself.

D SUTTON is not guilty of wasting police time as the cost did not exceed £25,000.

Question 11.5

MULLINS has been sold laminate flooring, which is defective, and has issued a county court claim against ACME Co. Ltd, who supplied the goods. CROCKETT is an expert laminate floor fitter and intends to give evidence on MULLIN's behalf at court. In order to prevent this, ACME's managing director have written a letter to CROCKETT warning him that he will lose business if he gives evidence against the company.

Does this letter amount to intimidation of a witness?

A Yes, provided there was intention to intimidate CROCKETT.

B Yes, provided the company were reckless as to whether CROCKETT would be intimidated.

C No, as the threat was not made in person.

D No, intimidating witnesses applies only to criminal court cases, not county court cases.

Question 11.6

LANEY is an accredited Police Community Support Officer (PCSO) and is dealing with ARMSTRONG for a fixed penalty offence. He requires ARMSTRONG to provide his name and address. ARMSTRONG refuses and LANEY exercises his power of detention as provided by sch. 4 to the Police Reform Act 2002. ARMSTRONG is less than impressed at this, and pushes the PCSO over and makes good his escape.

Consider the offence at common law of escaping. Which of the following is correct?

A ARMSTRONG has committed this offence. The offence is complete.

B ARMSTRONG has committed this offence provided he remains at liberty for at least 24 hours.

C ARMSTRONG has not committed this offence, as it relates to escaping from prisons, etc.

D ARMSTRONG has not committed this offence, and it relates to lawful custody, i.e. by a police officer.

Question 11.7

COOK is a potential juror at Crown Court. His wife works behind the bar of the 'Red Lion'. HUGHES, a friend of MAKINGS, who is about to stand trial for murder, enters the 'Red Lion' and approaches COOK's wife. HUGHES says, 'Tell your old man Makings is not guilty, or things could get very nasty for him and you'. HUGHES is intending to influence the jury in the case.

> Consider an offence under s. 51 of the Criminal Justice and Public Order Act 1994, intimidation of witnesses and jurors. Which of the following is true?
> A No offence; COOK is only a potential juror.
> B No offence as only a third party, the wife, was intimidated.
> C This is an offence, provided the wife felt threatened or intimidated.
> D This is an offence due to HUGHES' intention.

Question 11.8

Constable FORSYTH was working undercover driving a van in a drug smuggling operation and had assumed a new identity. This was more than just a false name; it amounted to identification and a legend outlining the false background of the identity she had assumed. Another officer, who was corrupt and under control of the main suspect in the drug smuggling, told the suspect that he believed that the person driving the van might have assumed a false identity, although he did not reveal the fact that she was an undercover police officer.

> Has the corrupt officer committed an offence of disclosing information relating to people assuming new identities contrary to the Serious Organised Crime and Police Act 2005, s. 88?
> A Yes the offence was committed when he revealed that the van driver had a false identity.
> B Yes, the offence was committed when he revealed that the van driver had a false identity knowing that the officer was 'a protected person'.
> C No, as he had not revealed that she was an undercover police officer and only in that role was she 'a protected person'.
> D No, whilst working undercover the undercover officer is not 'a protected person' within the definition of the 2005 Act.

Question 11.9

CHAPMAN was a witness in a trial at Crown Court. Two days before the trial he was approached by the defendant ALDUESCUE who pleaded with him to lie in court.

When CHAPMAN refused, ALDUESCUE became aggressive and threatened CHAP-MAN. CHAPMAN stated that he found the actions of the ALDUESCUE to have been intimidating, but that he himself did not feel intimidated, and he went on to give truthful evidence in court.

Has an offence of intimidating a witness been committed contrary to s. 51 of the Criminal Justice and Public Order Act 1994?

A   No, as CHAPMAN went on to give evidence in court.

B   No, as CHAPMAN was not actually intimidated.

C   Yes, but only because ALDUESCUE asked CHAPMAN to lie.

D   Yes, as ALDUESCUE has committed an act which intimidates.

Question 11.10

JACOBS attended a police station and made an allegation of rape against a taxi driver, who she stated had driven her home the previous evening. JACOBS said that she did not know the identity of the person who raped her and could not describe the taxi or the driver as she had been extremely intoxicated at the time. The police spent the next two days investigating the incident, but JACOBS later told them that she had made up the story because she had been late going home that night and she had a jealous boyfriend.

Would JACOBS' actions amount to an offence against the administration of justice and public interest in these circumstances?

A   No, because a course of justice had not commenced before JACOBS made the allegation.

B   No, because JACOBS did not identify any individual who may have been arrested or inconvenienced by her statement.

C   Yes, JACOBS' conduct could amount to perverting the course of justice, as there were possible consequences of detention, arrest, charge or prosecution.

D   Yes this could amount to an offence of wasting police time as over 24 hours police time had been used, but it could never be perverting the course of justice.

Question 11.11

CENA has been convicted of theft at Crown Court and given a custodial sentence. A private security company is responsible for transporting detainees to the local prison. Whilst en route to the prison McMANN rams the prison van with his Transit van and then overpowers the guards; subsequently he assists CENA to escape by unlocking his cell on the prison van.

Consider the offence of assisting escape contrary to the Prison Act 1952, s. 39 and McMANN's actions.

A   He commits the offence when he rams the prison van with the intention of assisting the escape.

B   He commits the offence only where he physically assisted the escape by unlocking the cell.

C   He does not commit the offence as it relates only to escape from police or prison transport, not from a private security company.

D   He does not commit this offence as it does not relate to prisoners in transit to or from prison.

ANSWERS

Answer 11.1

Answer **D** — Section 1(1) of the Perjury Act 1911 states:

If any person lawfully sworn as a witness or as an interpreter in a judicial proceeding wilfully makes a statement material in that proceeding, which he knows to
be false or does not believe to be true, he shall be guilty of perjury...

'Any person' includes the defendant and therefore answer A is incorrect. There
is no requirement to show intention to mislead the court; simply making the statement deliberately is enough, and therefore answer C is incorrect. It is possible for a
witness or interpreter to make a solemn affirmation in place of the oath, whether
or not the taking of an oath would be contrary to his or her religious beliefs, and s.
15(2) of the Perjury Act 1911 provides that references therein to 'oaths' and 'swearing' embrace affirmations. The affirming witness is therefore equally subject to the
Perjury Act 1911 and answer B is also incorrect.

Crime, para. 1.15.2

Answer 11.2

Answer **C** — The offence of assisting offenders applies only where a relevant offence has been committed. A 'relevant offence' means —

(a) an offence for which the sentence is fixed by law,
(b) an offence for which a person of 18 years or over (not previously convicted) may be
    sentenced to imprisonment for a term of five years (or might be so sentenced but
    for the restrictions imposed by section 33 of the Magistrates' Courts Act 1980).

The offence committed here is summary only and therefore answer A is incorrect.

The Serious Organised Crime and Police Act 2005, sch. 7, part 3 contains amendments consequential on the repeal of the definitions and concepts of an 'arrestable
offence' and a 'serious arrestable offence'. In general, this will mean that police
powers which were available in cases involving 'serious arrestable offences' and 'arrestable offences' will now only be available in cases involving indictable only or
triable either way offences.

Harbouring offenders applies to people who have escaped from a prison or other
institutions, and therefore answer B is incorrect. The sister has almost certainly committed an offence of perverting the course of public justice and, arguably, wasting

police time, under s. 5(2) of the Criminal Law Act 1967; answer D is therefore incorrect.

Crime, paras 1.15.7, 1.15.9

Answer 11.3

Answer **A** — Common law corruption is described in *R v Bembridge* (1783) 3 Doug 327: '[a] man accepting an office of trust concerning the public is answerable criminally to the [the Crown] for misbehaviour in his office...by whomever and in whatever way the officer is appointed'. In *R v Bowden* [1996] 1 WLR 98, the Court of Appeal held that a local authority manager, who improperly arranged for his men to carry out work at his girlfriend's house, was guilty of the offence of common law corruption. Public bodies corruption is defined in the Public Bodies Corrupt Practices Act 1889 as 'every person who shall by himself or by or in conjunction with any other person, corruptly solicit or receive, or agree to receive, for himself, or for any other person, any gift, loan, fee, reward, or advantage', which is not the case here so answer B is incorrect. Corruption of agents is described in the Prevention of Corruption Act 1906 as 'if any agent corruptly accepts or obtains, or agrees to accept or attempts to obtain, from any person, for himself or for any other person, any gift or consideration as an inducement or reward', which again is not the case here, so answer C is incorrect. As an offence has been committed, answer D is incorrect.

Crime, paras 1.15.12.1, 1.15.12.2

Answer 11.4

Answer **B** — The definition of this offence (Criminal Law Act 1967, s. 5(2)) includes the phrase 'making to any person a false report' and therefore answer C is incorrect. Contrary to popular belief, there is no time limit for this offence, and answer A is also incorrect. Likewise, there is no monetary value placed on this offence and therefore answer D is incorrect.

Crime, para. 1.15.10

Answer 11.5

Answer **A** — Section 39 of the Criminal Justice and Police Act 2001 extended the offences of intimidation of witness offences outlined in s. 51 of the Criminal Justice and Public Order Act 1994 to proceedings in civil cases. The 1994 Act applies to the investigation or trial of those in criminal proceedings. Answer D is therefore in-correct. The new offence is very similar to the 1994 Act offence and is an offence of specific intent, so recklessness will not suffice (answer B is therefore incorrect). The offence includes doing any act, provided it was with the intention of intimid-ating a witness and provided the defendant knew the person might be a witness. This would include writing letters, making phone calls, etc., and is not limited to personal threats (answer C is also incorrect).

Crime, para. 1.15.5.2

Answer 11.6

Answer **A** — This offence applies to persons in lawful custody, anywhere. It is not restricted to custody units, prison, etc. Answer C is therefore incorrect. Whether a person is 'in custody' or not is a question of fact and the word 'custody' is to be given its ordinary meaning (*E v DPP* [2002] Crime LR 737). This could be shown by providing evidence that the person's liberty was restricted (as it is in the ques-tion), and that it was lawful (sch. 4 to the 2002 Act provides this). This custody is not restricted to sworn police officers and would include police community support officers (PCSOs), Investigating Officers or Escort Officers (who are given powers by the 2002 Act); answer D is therefore incorrect. The offence of escaping is completed immediately that liberty is obtained and is not subject to time restrictions on such liberty; therefore, answer B is incorrect.

Crime, para. 1.15.9

Answer 11.7

Answer **D** — Section 51 deals with intimidation of witnesses and jurors:

(1) A person commits an offence if —
 (a) he does an act which intimidates, and is intended to intimidate, another person ('the victim'),
 (b) he does the act knowing or believing that the victim is assisting in the invest-igation of an offence or is a witness or potential witness or a juror or potential juror in proceedings for an offence, and
 (c) he does it intending thereby to cause the investigation or the course of justice to be obstructed, perverted or interfered with.

It includes potential jurors; therefore answer A is incorrect. This is a crime of spe-cific intent, and it makes no difference what the outcome of the intimidation is, provided the relevant intent is present; answer C is therefore incorrect. The offence can be committed against a person other than the victim, as outlined in s. 51(3):

> For the purposes of subsections (1) and (2) it is immaterial that the act is or would be done, or that the threat is made —
> (a) otherwise than in the presence of the victim, or
> (b) to a person other than the victim.

Answer B is therefore incorrect.

Crime, para. 1.15.5.1

Answer 11.8

Answer **D** — Chapter 4 of the Serious Organised Crime and Police Act 2005 allows for the making of arrangements to protect these and other relevant people ordinarily resident in the UK where the 'protection provider' (usually the Chief Officer of Police or the Director General of the Serious Organised Crime Agency) considers that the person's safety is at risk by virtue of their being a witness, constable, juror etc. (s. 82(1)). This included providing that person with a new identity, and this person is further protected by s. 88 of the 2005 Act, which makes it an offence to disclose information relating to people assuming new identities. You would need to show that the defendant made the disclosure and that they had the relevant knowledge or suspicion (that the person assumed, or might have assumed, a new identity).

The new identity adopted by the protected person must have been in pursuance of arrangements made under s. 82(1). Therefore if a witness simply takes it on themselves to assume a new name without any involvement by the protection provider, the above offences will not apply. Similarly, this offence will not generally apply where the identity is one that has been adopted by an undercover officer in the course of his/her duties. So as reprehensible as the corrupt officer's actions were he did not commit an offence contrary to s. 88 of the Serious Organised Crime and Police Act 2005; answers A, B and C are therefore incorrect.

Crime, para. 1.15.5

Answer 11.9

Answer **D** — The Criminal Justice and Public Order Act 1994, s. 51 states:

> (1) A person commits an offence if —
> (a) he does an act which intimidates, and is intended to intimidate, another person ('the victim')...

In a decision that seems to contradict the specific wording above the Court of Appeal held, *inter alia*, that intimidation does not have to be successful, in that the victim does not actually have to be deterred from giving evidence or put in fear. Answers A and B are therefore incorrect. Whilst it will be material evidence if the victim was neither deterred from giving evidence nor put in fear, a person may intimidate another person without the victim being intimidated (*R v Patrascu* [2004] EWCA Crim 2417). Note that this section extends well beyond simply asking a person to lie, and can include other ways of obstructing justice through witness intimidation. Answer C is therefore incorrect.

Crime, para. 1.15.5.1

Answer 11.10

Answer **C** — It is an offence at common law to do an act tending and intended to pervert the course of public justice. 'The course of public justice' includes the process of criminal investigation (see *R v Rowell* (1977) 65 Cr App R 174) — it is not necessary that an investigation has commenced *before* the person makes a false complaint, such as the one above. Answer A is therefore incorrect.

The conduct referred to in the scenario *may* amount to an offence of wasting police time (contrary to s. 5 of the Criminal Law Act 1967), although contrary to popular belief there is no minimum number of hours which must be wasted before a prosecution can be brought for this offence. However it has also been held to amount to perverting the course of justice, (see *R v Goodwin* (1989) 11 Cr App R (S) 194, where a false allegation of rape was made to the police). Answer D is therefore incorrect.

Where a person makes a false allegation to the police justifying a criminal investigation with the possible consequences of detention, arrest, charge or prosecution, and that person intends that the allegation be taken seriously, the offence of perverting the course of justice is *prima facie* made out. This will be the case *whether or not the allegation is capable of identifying specific individuals*, (see *R v Cotter* [2002] 2 Cr App R 29, a case involving the boyfriend of a well-known black Olympic athlete who falsely claimed to have been attacked as part of a racist campaign). Answer B is therefore incorrect.

Crime, para. 1.15.4

Answer 11.11

Answer **D** — The Prison Act 1952, s. 39 states:

Any person who aids any prisoner in escaping or attempting to escape from a prison or who, with intent to facilitate the escape of any prisoner, sends anything (by post or otherwise) into a prison or to a prisoner or places any thing anywhere outside a prison with a view to its coming into the possession of a prisoner, shall be guilty of [an offence].

The wording of the section seems to indicate that it only relates to 'escaping' from a prison, and this was verified by the Court of Appeal in *R* v *Moss and Harte* (1986) 82 Cr App R 116 where it was held that the offence under s. 39 of the 1952 Act does not apply to a prisoner who escapes while in transit to or from prison; answers A, B and C are therefore incorrect.

Crime, para. 1.15.9

12 Offences Arising from Immigration, Asylum and People Exploitation

STUDY PREPARATION

This chapter deals with one of the most contentious policing issues of modern times, that of illegal entry to the United Kingdom. The events of 11 September 2001 prompted swift and considerable changes to immigration offences throughout the world. Immigration, asylum and exploitation of people has become an increasingly significant area of criminal activity in Wales and England, and central government has been swift to react with legislative changes to deal with the escalating problem. The unlawful exploitation of vulnerable people has, as it should be, been a priority; legislation dealing with that is tested here.

QUESTIONS

Question 12.1

KANG is originally from Pakistan, but is now a British citizen. His brother (who is not a British citizen) wishes to come to Britain on a permanent basis, but has falsely filled out an entry application stating he is coming on holiday. KANG has signed this form to say that his brother will stay with him on holiday for two weeks. KANG knows this to be false.

Who, if either, commits an offence under s. 24A of the Immigration Act 1971?

A KANG only, as a British citizen.

B Both KANG and his brother.

C His brother only, as he is not a British citizen.

D Neither, this offence applies only to applications for citizenship.

Question 12.2

It is an offence under s. 36 of the Criminal Justice Act 1925 to make an untrue statement to procure a passport.

> In relation to this offence, which of the following is true in relation to the person making that statement?

A That he makes the statement believing it not to be true.

B That he makes the statement knowing or believing it not to be true.

C That he makes the statement and is reckless as to whether it is true or not.

D That the statement is to his knowledge untrue.

Question 12.3

Under s. 2 of the Asylum and Immigration (Treatment of Claimants etc.) Act 2004, a person will commit an offence if, when at a leave or asylum interview, he/she does not have with him/her a passport or other document establishing his/her nationality or citizenship.

> Section 2(3) of the Act provides a time period, during which a person may produce the passport or document, to avoid prosecution for the offence. In relation to this period, when must the passport or document be produced?

A Within 24 hours.

B Within 2 days.

C Within 3 days.

D Within 7 days.

Question 12.4

GREER owns a warehouse which processes fresh fish and shellfish. The product is caught locally and then sold on to small businesses in a local coastal town. GREER has formed a relationship with SOWDEN, who supplies workers to the warehouse during the summer months, when business increases due to tourism. GREER is aware that SOWDEN does not have a license to procure the workers' services, but being grateful for the extra help, asks no questions. GREER pays the workers a minimum wage, but does not pay SOWDEN for supplying them.

Would GREER be guilty of an offence under the Gangmasters (Licensing) Act 2004?

A No, because the workers are not gathering produce.

B No, only SOWDEN commits an offence, by supplying the workers.

C No, because the workers are paid for their services.

D Yes, GREER commits an offence by entering into an arrangement with SOWDEN.

Question 12.5

The Gangmasters (Licensing) Act 2004 regulates certain aspects of unlawful exploitation of vulnerable groups of people within England and Wales, in relation to work that they are expected to do.

Which of the below is *specifically* listed in the definition of 'work', contained in s. 3 of the Act?

A Working in restaurants or takeaways.

B Prostitution.

C Agricultural work.

D Manual labour on building sites etc.

Question 12.6

It is an offence under s. 4 of the Asylum and Immigration (Treatment of Claimants etc.) Act 2004 to traffic people for exploitation.

The definition of exploitation can be found in s. 4(4) of the Act. Which of the following is *specifically* listed in the definition?

A Exploiting a person for the purposes of organ transplants.

B Exploiting a person for the purpose of prostitution.

C Exploiting a person for the purpose of enforced marriage.

D Exploiting a person for the purpose of child pornography.

Question 12.7

RAYMOND is a transport manager for a haulage company, which operates in the UK and Europe. RAYMOND is aware that several of his drivers transport illegal immigrants into the UK. However, because his role includes allocating workloads, he is often asked by drivers to swap routes at the last minute. RAYMOND suspects that the drivers request these changes to allow them to pick up people, but he turns a blind eye and generally accedes to their requests. RAYMOND is not involved in any of the arrangements, but he believes that most of the people transported may be exploited by being used as cheap labour, for which they will not be paid.

Would RAYMOND be guilty of an offence under s. 4 of the Asylum and Immigration (Treatment of Claimants etc.) Act 2004 (trafficking people for exploitation)?

A Yes, but only if it can be shown that he holds more than a mere belief that the people will be exploited.

B No, because he does not arrange to transport the people.

C Yes, he would be guilty of the offence in these circumstances alone.

D No, because he is not directly involved in the exploitation of people.

Question 12.8

HALL and CARTER were both British citizens and were taking an extended holiday in Spain, staying on CARTER's yacht. HALL met and fell in love with ALLONSO, a Spanish citizen, and they decided they could not be apart when HALL was due to return to Britain. ALLONSO was deported from the UK some two years previously but has not told either HALL or CARTER and she persuades HALL to go back to the UK on the yacht and therefore avoid immigration. HALL believes as an EU member state national there would be no problem in ALLONSO arriving in this manner, and CARTER agrees to the use of his yacht for this purpose. HALL unfortunately does not have good sea legs and has to fly back to the UK. CARTER and ALLONSO arrive at Brixham in Devon on the yacht and are met there by HALL after they had disembarked from the yacht.

Which of the following statements is correct, in respect of the offence of assisting entry to the United Kingdom in breach of a deportation order contrary to the Immigration Act 1971, s. 25B?

A Only CARTER commits the offence, as the person who actually brought ALLONSO into the country.

B Only HALL commits the offence, as it was his scheme to bring ALLONSO to the UK by this method.

C Both HALL and CARTER commit the offence as they colluded together to assist ALLONSO's arrival.

D Neither HALL nor CARTER commit the offence in these circumstances.

Question 12.9

DAYNI is an Iraqi national who wishes to enter Britain, and gets as far as France. There he meets other persons who also wish to gain illegal entry into Britain. DAYNI is introduced to PRESCOTT, a French national, who agrees to help DAYNI and gives him a false passport and arranges for him to be smuggled in, in the back of a lorry.

Considering the offence of assisting unlawful immigration to member states (contrary to s. 25 of the Immigration Act 1971), which of the following is correct?

A PRESCOTT commits the offence only because he gave DAYNI a false passport.

B PRESCOTT commits the offence when he gives DAYNI a false passport, and also when he arranges transportation.

C PRESCOTT does not commit the offence because he was outside the United Kingdom when he helped DAYNI.

D PRESCOTT does not commit the offence because he himself is not a British citizen.

Question 12.10

FAHDAWI is an asylum seeker and has been issued with a registration card by the secretary of state. FAHDAWI notices after a few weeks that his date of birth on the card is incorrect. Not wishing to make a fuss he changes the last number of his date of birth himself.

Has FAHDAWI committed an offence of misuse of a registration card contrary to the Immigration Act 1971, s. 26A?

A Yes, it is an offence to alter any detail contained on a registration card.

B Yes, although the holder can amend some details it is an offence to alter any personal details on a registration card.

C No, there was no intention to deceive and this is required for the offence to be committed.

D No, as the change was merely as the result of a mistake by the card issuer no offence is committed.

ANSWERS

Answer 12.1

Answer **C** — Section 24A of the Immigration Act 1971 is aimed at the actions of non-British citizens only, so as a British citizen, KANG can never commit this offence (answers A and B are incorrect). It applies to any application to obtain or seek to obtain leave to enter the UK in any circumstances, including holidays, and therefore answer D is incorrect. KANG's brother commits the offence as he uses means which include deception to achieve his leave to enter.

Crime, para. 1.16.2.4

Answer 12.2

Answer **D** — The offence is made out where the person who makes the statement does so in the knowledge that it is untrue. His beliefs and actions in relation to checking the veracity of the statement are of no consequence. What is important is that he knows the statement he made is untrue. Answers A, B and C are therefore incorrect.

Crime, para. 1.16.5

Answer 12.3

Answer **C** — The passport or document must be provided to an immigration officer or to the Secretary of State within a period of *three* days, beginning with the date of that interview. Answers A, B and D are therefore incorrect.

Crime, para. 1.16.5

Answer 12.4

Answer **D** — An unlicensed gangmaster is a person who illegally supplies people to conduct the work listed in s. 3 of the Gangmasters (Licensing) Act 2004. The work listed in this section is essentially agricultural work, gathering shellfish *and includes* processing or packaging any produce derived from agricultural work, shellfish, fish or products derived from shellfish or fish. Answer A is therefore incorrect.

Section 6 of the Act makes provision for licences to be issued by the Gangmasters Licensing Authority (GLA) to suitable persons. It is an offence to act as a gangmaster without a licence (see. s. 12(1)). It is a further summary offence to enter into an arrangement with a gangmaster where, in supplying the workers or services, the gangmaster contravenes s. 6 (s. 13(1)). Answer B is therefore incorrect. Lastly, it is irrelevant that the workers were paid for their services — the offence is complete when GREER enters into an arrangement with SOWDEN. Answer C is therefore incorrect.

Crime, para. 1.16.3.4

Answer 12.5

Answer **C** — The deaths of 23 illegal immigrants in Morecambe Bay in February 2004 drew attention to unlawful exploitation of vulnerable groups of people within England and Wales. On that occasion, the illegal workers were gathering shellfish. A gangmaster is a person who illegally supplies people to conduct the work listed in s. 3 of the Gangmasters (Licensing) Act 2004. The work listed in this section is essentially agricultural work, gathering shellfish and includes processing or packaging any produce derived from agricultural work, shellfish, fish or products derived from shellfish or fish. Answers A, B and D are therefore incorrect.

Crime, para. 1.16.3.4

Answer 12.6

Answer **A** — The definition of exploitation under s. 4(4) is fairly wide and includes where a person is:

- a victim of the Human Rights Convention — slavery and forced labour;
- encouraged, required or expected to do anything as a result of which they (or another person) would commit an offence under the Human Organ Transplants Act 1989;
- subjected to force, threats or deception designed to induce them to provide services, provide another person with benefits or enable another person to acquire benefits of any kind;
- requested or induced to undertake *any activity* having been chosen on the grounds they are mentally or physically ill or disabled, young or have a family relationship with a person and a person without the illness, disability, youth or family relationship would be likely to refuse the request or resist the inducement.

Of the choices in this question, only exploiting a person for the purposes of organ transplants appears specifically in the list. Therefore answers B, C and D are incorrect. However, any of the other scenarios may fall within the offence, depending on the circumstances.

Crime, para. 1.16.3.3

Answer 12.7

Answer **C** — An offence is committed under s. 4(1) of the Asylum and Immigration (Treatment of Claimants etc.) Act 2004, when a person arranges *or* facilitates the arrival in the UK of an individual (the 'passenger'). The dictionary definition of 'facilitate' includes to 'smooth the progress of', 'make easy', or 'make possible'. Even though RAYMOND is not directly involved in the arrangements, he could certainly be accused of facilitating the arrival of the passengers. Answer B is therefore incorrect.

Section 4(1) continues that the person will be guilty of the offence, if he/she:

(a) intends to exploit the passenger in the UK or elsewhere, *or*
(b) *believes another person* is likely to exploit the passenger in the UK or elsewhere.

Therefore, even though RAYMOND is not directly involved in the exploitation of the passengers, he commits the offence because of his belief that they will be exploited (and answer D is incorrect). Answer A is incorrect because the prosecution would have to show a *belief* by the accused and no more. The definition of 'exploitation' under s. 4(4) includes where a person is victim of Article 4 of the Human Rights Convention — slavery and forced labour.

It should be noted that there are further offences contained in s. 4, namely, arranging or facilitating the travel within the UK of a passenger, with the same intent (s. 4(2)), and arranging or facilitating the *departure* from UK of above person with the same intent (s. 4(3)).

Crime, para. 1.16.3.3

Answer 12.8

Answer **D** — An offence of assisting entry to the United Kingdom in breach of deportation order contrary to the Immigration Act 1971, s. 25B is committed *inter alia* where the defendant does an act which assists the individual to arrive in, enter or remain in the United Kingdom, and that person is subject to a deportation order.

The defendant must have known or had reasonable cause for believing that their act facilitated assisting the entry in breach of that deportation order, therefore they must have known/had reasonable cause to believe that there was such an order in existence. As in the scenario neither man knew of the deportation order they commit no offence; answers A, B and C are therefore incorrect.

It should be noted that ALLONSO, however, may be guilty of an offence under s. 24(1)(a) of the 1971 Act, of being a person who is not a British citizen who knowingly enters the UK in breach of a deportation order or without leave.

Crime, para. 1.16.3.1

Answer 12.9

Answer **D** — Section 25 of the Immigration Act 1971 is a very broadly worded offence, which requires that the defendant facilitated the commission of any breach of immigration law by someone who is not an EU citizen. This would include actions clearly facilitating the entry, such as furnishing the person with a false passport, but also less apparent help, such as organising transport into the UK; answer A is therefore incorrect.

Although this offence can be committed outside the United Kingdom, it can only be committed by British citizens and others with relevant forms of British citizenship. As PRESCOTT is not a British citizen he will not commit this offence.

Hands up all those who missed where it said that he was a French national!

Crime, para. 1.16.3.1

Answer 12.10

Answer **C** — The Immigration Act 1971, s. 26A states:

(3) A person commits an offence if he —
    (a) makes a false registration card,
    (b) alters a registration card with intent to deceive or to enable another to deceive
      ...

A registration card here is a document which:

- carries information about a person (whether or not wholly or partly electronically); and
- is issued by the Secretary of State to the person wholly or partly in connection with a claim for asylum (whether or not made by that person)

(s. 26A(1)).

These offences require different degrees of intent and the wording of each needs to be considered carefully and they are similar to the more general offences of forgery. In this scenario although he altered the card there was no intent to deceive or to enable another to deceive and therefore there is no offence; answers A, B and D are therefore incorrect.

Crime, para. 1.16.4

Question Checklist

The checklist below is designed to help you keep track of your progress when answering the multiple-choice questions. If you fill this in after one attempt at each question, you will be able to check how many you have got right and which questions you need to revisit a second time. Also available on-line, to download visit: www.blackstonespolicemanuals.com.

	First attempt Correct (✓)	Second attempt Correct (✓)
1 State of Mind and Criminal Conduct		
1.1		
1.2		
1.3		
1.4		
1.5		
1.6		
1.7		
1.8		
1.9		
1.10		
1.11		
1.12		
1.13		
1.14		
1.15		
1.16		
2 Incomplete Offences and Police Investigations		
2.1		
2.2		
2.3		
2.4		

	First attempt Correct (✓)	Second attempt Correct (✓)
2.5		
2.6		
2.7		
2.8		
2.9		
2.10		
2.11		
2.12		
3 General Defences		
3.1		
3.2		
3.3		
3.4		
3.5		
3.6		
3.7		
3.8		
3.9		
3.10		
3.11		
3.12		
3.13		
3.14		

	First attempt Correct (✓)	Second attempt Correct (✓)
4 Homicide		
4.1		
4.2		
4.3		
4.4		
4.5		
4.6		
4.7		
4.8		
4.9		
4.10		
5 Misuse of Drugs		
5.1		
5.2		
5.3		
5.4		
5.5		
5.6		
5.7		
5.8		
5.9		
5.10		
5.11		
5.12		
5.13		
5.14		
5.15		
5.16		
5.17		
5.18		
5.19		
6 Offences Against the Person		
6.1		
6.2		
6.3		
6.4		
6.5		

	First attempt Correct (✓)	Second attempt Correct (✓)
6.6		
6.7		
6.8		
6.9		
6.10		
6.11		
6.12		
6.13		
6.14		
6.15		
6.16		
6.17		
6.18		
6.19		
7 Sexual Offences		
7.1		
7.2		
7.3		
7.4		
7.5		
7.6		
7.7		
7.8		
7.9		
7.10		
7.11		
7.12		
7.13		
7.14		
7.15		
7.16		
7.17		
7.18		
7.19		
7.20		
7.21		
7.22		
7.23		

	First attempt Correct (✓)	Second attempt Correct (✓)
7.24		
7.25		
7.26		
7.27		
7.28		
7.29		
8 Child Protection		
8.1		
8.2		
8.3		
8.4		
8.5		
8.6		
8.7		
8.8		
8.9		
8.10		
8.11		
9 Offences Amounting to Dishonesty, Deception and Fraud		
9.1		
9.2		
9.3		
9.4		
9.5		
9.6		
9.7		
9.8		
9.9		
9.10		
9.11		
9.12		
9.13		
9.14		
9.15		
9.16		
9.17		
9.18		

	First attempt Correct (✓)	Second attempt Correct (✓)
9.19		
9.20		
9.21		
9.22		
9.23		
9.24		
9.25		
9.26		
9.27		
9.28		
9.29		
9.30		
10 Criminal Damage		
10.1		
10.2		
10.3		
10.4		
10.5		
10.6		
10.7		
10.8		
10.9		
10.10		
10.11		
10.12		
11 Offences Against the Administration of Justice and Public Interest		
11.1		
11.2		
11.3		
11.4		
11.5		
11.6		
11.7		
11.8		
11.9		
11.10		

	First attempt Correct (✓)	Second attempt Correct (✓)
11.11		
12 Offences Arising from Immigration, Asylum and People Exploitation		
12.1		
12.2		
12.3		
12.4		

	First attempt Correct (✓)	Second attempt Correct (✓)
12.5		
12.6		
12.7		
12.8		
12.9		
12.10		

Be Prepared!

Essential ONLINE study-aids for all police officers sitting the Part I promotion examinations

Fully updated for the 2007 syllabus

Blackstone's Police Q&As Online

- An online **Multiple Choice Questions database** which offers all the exam practice you need to maximise your chances of success
- **Over 1400 questions**—all of the same format and difficulty as the actual exam
- Choose the number of questions you want to do **from 10 questions**, to a **whole mock exam**
- Study questions from a **single subject** or a **mixture of all four**
- Get **detailed feedback** on your performance and a full user history
- **Answers are fully explained and cross-referenced** to the Blackstone's Police Manuals so you can easily go back and revise the relevant subject area

Subscriptions: **£95.00** (12 months) | **£75.00** (8 months) | **£50.00** (3 months)

Blackstone's Police Manuals Online

- **Fast, desktop access** to the complete text of all four Blackstone's Police Manuals
- Find the information you need quickly and easily by using the **powerful search engine** via the table of contents or the consolidated A–Z index
- Extensive **cross-referencing** ensures you can easily revise all relevant subject areas together
- **Endorsed by CENTREX** and written in consultation with police forces across England and Wales

Subscriptions: **£78.00** (12 months) | **£58.00** (8 months)

Blackstone's Police Manuals and Q&As Online

Subscriptions: **£150.00** (12 months) | **£120.00** (8 months)

For more information and subscription details, please visit **www.blackstonespolice.com**

Please note the Blackstone's Police Q&As Online service is not endorsed by Centrex

ALBQ&AA07

Also available to help with your revision

Blackstone's Police Sergeants' and Inspectors' Mock Examination Paper 2007

Paul Connor, *Police Trainer*

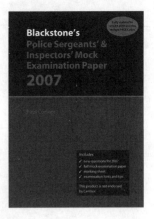

'Hits straight at the heart of the matter in a no nonsense fashion.'

Detective Sergeant Simon Davies, West Mercia Police

'The student will learn not only the answers, but also the process by using this product.'

Detective Sergeant Phil Stokoe, Durham Police

Minimise last-minute panic and increase your confidence with this one-stop resource for examination technique and practice.

- Test your knowledge of the *Blackstone's Police Manuals 2007* by answering 150 questions in 3 hours.
- Packed with handy hints and practical tips to prepare you for the examination day.
- Check your answers and use the handy references to the relevant parts of the *Blackstone's Police Manuals 2007* to follow up your mock exam with targeted revision.

Blackstone's Police Sergeants' and Inspectors' Mock Examination Paper 2007 features a selection of multiple-choice questions set by an experienced question writer. Designed for use in simulated exam conditions, it will test your knowledge and understanding of the law, and your ability to answer questions under pressure.

The mock examination paper is accompanied by detailed marking matrices; allowing you to calculate your overall percentage score and recognize the areas you need to focus on. Learn where your areas of strength and weakness lie, and channel your revision into the most productive areas of the syllabus.

Applicable to the Sergeants' Part I promotion exam in March 2007 and the Inspectors' exam in September 2007.

For more information on this, and other Police books from Blackstone's, please visit **www.oup.co.uk/law/police**

£14.99   Available from all good bookshops

October 2006 | 110 pages | Paperback | 0-19-920733-X / 978-0-19-920733-6

Please note this product is not endorsed by Centrex